CITY SIGNALS

Principles and Practices for **Ministering in Today's Global Communities**

Brad Smith

NEW HOPE
PUBLISHERS

BIRMINGHAM, ALABAMA

New Hope® Publishers
P. O. Box 12065
Birmingham, AL 35202-2065
www.newhopepublishers.com

New Hope Publishers is a division of WMU®.

Library of Congress Cataloging-in-Publication Data

Smith, Brad, 1959-
  City signals : principles and practices for ministering in today's
global communities / by Brad Smith.
    p. cm.
  ISBN 978-1-59669-045-5 (sc)
  1. City churches. 2. City missions. 3. Pastoral theology. I. Title.
  BV637.S57 2008
  259.09173'2--dc22

                    2008012901

ISBN-10: 1-59669-045-3
ISBN-13: 978-1-59669-045-5

N074130 • 0808 • 4M1

DEDICATION

City Signals is dedicated to my wife, Debby, and our children, Virginia, Laws, and Macrae, who have joined me on this global urban adventure. I also want to express my gratitude to the Bakke Graduate University learning community of board members, regents, staff, students, and faculty, who are constantly teaching me new things in their home cities throughout the world.

CONTENTS

PREFACE

This is a study about exploding growth and prominence of global cities in our world. It is designed for people who minister within their community and city. You may be a long-time veteran or a new explorer of city ministry. You may be working with the urban poor or the urban powerful. You may be a church volunteer in a ghetto or a CEO of a business providing products to meet strategic needs in the city. You may have grown up in the "hood" and are leading your lifelong family and friends to improve your street, or you may live in the suburbs and drive each week to the city to be with new friends. You may be focused on a few people, a neighborhood, or an overall strategy to transform your city's social structures of government, economy, and infrastructure. Whatever you are doing, you are participating in activities that often are called *urban ministry, community development*, or *city transformation*. If so, we hope this study will give you new ideas and tools to pursue your calling in the city.

How to Use *City Signals*

This study is designed to introduce you to key spiritual formation processes you can explore regarding urban ministry. *City Signals* can be read individually and in a group as a reflection that serves the following people:
- a church leader considering the costs and benefits of increasing the church's involvement in local urban missions
- the staff of an urban ministry organization planning either a weekend retreat or weekly Bible studies
- a small group of individuals in a suburban church that has decided to do more community ministry in its own city

- a short-term missions team preparing itself as a community before leaving for an urban mission experience
- students preparing for an urban plunge
- students in a course on urban ministry

This study also identifies core urban ministry principles that are also illustrated with the *City Signals* DVD series in a special *City Signals* leader's kit.

City Signals Leaders Kit

These DVDs are vignettes of various aspects of urban ministry. They include ten segments, about 25-minutes, each that feature urbanologist, missiologist, and acclaimed Bible teacher Ray Bakke sharing about the core principles of urban ministry. Filmed and coproduced with Mark Joeckel, the DVD series came in response to a question I asked Ray; "After 30 years and hundreds of talks on urban ministry, what have you learned that you think anyone entering urban ministry should know?" We have added a Leader's Guide to provide structure for group discussion of the DVD content.

The book and DVD flexible structure make it possible for small-group leaders and other teachers to pull out and rearrange the chapters into the order that best serves their group's needs. Individuals also can focus a personal study on the book chapters and end-of-chapter questions, or can use both book and the leader's kit.

The DVD series includes two presentations entitled, *Saints in Cities: An Urban Family Album of the Past 2000 Years*. These two segments provide a whirlwind tour of urban themes in church history as told through key personalities in that history. Consider this an encore presentation to the first eight sessions that can be used to continue learning about the amazing history of God's work over the past 2,000 years in the city.

The DVD series introduces you to the key subject themes of urban ministry. Used together with the *City Signals* book in a group setting, it is hoped the series prepares minds and hearts for what God has in store for urban ministers.

INTRODUCTION

Red traffic lights are a nuisance. They make us wait. They make our trips longer. They waste so much of our time.

Some emergency vehicles are equipped with remote control devices to get rid of red lights. The ambulance driver can push a button and all the lights along a street turn green as a signal from the ambulance indicates it is drawing near an intersection.

I would love to have one of those buttons. I would gain time by not having to wait for red lights. I would arrive where I wanted to be, ahead of time and in such a better mood. I could get so much more done. I would be so much happier. What a difference it would make to have that device in my car—as long as no one else in my city had one too.

Yet cities cannot work without red lights. A red light from our viewpoint is actually a green light from someone else's viewpoint. To get *our* way, sometimes we have to yield to others, to get *their* way. Red lights remind us that there is a higher authority in our city called the Transportation Board that is determining how we are all going to get along with each other as we drive our cars.

There is much about red lights that parallels how God creates growing disciples of Jesus Christ. There are three ways to attempt to avoid these red lights:

(1) *Run through them.* Sooner or later, however, the consequences would be painful or even deadly to us and others.

(2) *Avoid driving*. However, our lives wouldn't be as rich.

(3) *Leave the city*: Deep in the countryside, there are more open roads and fewer red lights, but also much less opportunity for relationships and community.

Each of the three ways to avoid red lights leads us away from health, a diverse life, and community. If we want the benefits derived from those aspects of life, we also must have red lights. We have a choice. Are the benefits of avoiding an accident, driving a car, and living in the city worth the inconvenience of red lights? Urban ministry is about similar choices.

Red Light, Green Light

Many people from the suburbs have briefly tasted how urban ministry adds spiritual health, a diverse life, and a growing community to their lives. Within urban ministry they've found a new awareness of their dependence on God as they are faced with people and situations that they don't understand and that no amount of money or organization can fix. They have been fascinated as they see the world through "eyes" that are culturally, economically, socially, and geographically different than their own. They have experienced the thrill of being able to help others in concrete ways. They have found deep friendships and even an odd sense of belonging in the urban world—that they don't find in their own suburban world.

Others have grown up in the city and minister in the place of their roots. When they have attempted to move to the suburbs, the pristine malls, rich green lawns, and high fences that looked so good at first slowly grow to look like so much plastic. The smells, sights, and people of the suburbs seem muted in comparison to the pungent odors and chaotic colors of the city. The open spaces of the countryside seem lonely compared to the cramped alleys.

This book is for people who are increasingly fascinated with the city and know there is no other place for them. It is a guide for individuals or groups who have experienced the thrill of the *green* lights of urban ministry, and who are frustrated with the red lights. Most people, even those in short-term urban ministry, quickly wonder why there are so many aspects of urban ministry that feel so inefficient, painful, and futile—like a street full of red lights.

This book is not a "how to" book to learn how to avoid red lights. In fact, a reoccurring theme you will see is that to avoid red lights is to avoid God's best. What it will attempt to do is to celebrate both the green and red lights in new ways. The city is a kaleidoscope of rich relationships, learning, and joy unlike any other. The city is our gateway to seeing the whole world unlike ever before. We will see how God sees the city as the ultimate place of blessing, even if people who don't understand the city, call it a curse. We will understand that the urban *mind-set* is a powerful force for growing disciples, even in the suburbs or countryside.

As you've already suspected, red lights are a necessary part of growing as a disciple. The goal of a disciple is freedom that comes from submission to God; health that comes from avoiding selfish convenience; and joy that comes from serving. The logic of a disciple's journey is upside-down from the logic of pursuing recognition, increasing ministry efficiency, or gaining personal significance. The logic of red lights in disciple-making is somewhat odd. The more red lights you have as a disciple, the faster you get to your destination! There are few places that provide more red lights to hurry you in your discipleship journey than the city does.

> "Consider it pure joy, my brothers, whenever you face trials of many kinds, because you know that the testing of your faith develops perseverance. Perseverance must finish its work so that you may be mature and complete, not lacking anything."
>
> —JAMES 1:2–4 (NIV)

Chapter One: OUR STORY IN THE CITY

Spiritual Formation Principle #1: Spiritual formation starts with God's story of joy and brokenness in our life.

Theme: The city is an amazing place of beauty, blessing, and fulfillment for those who have ready eyes to see it that way. It is also a place that draws and forms those who are willing to explore what it means to be *broken* before God.

Bible Reading: Psalm 107
Pay particular attention to the phrases:
- "Those he gathered from the lands, from east and west, from north and south" (v. 3).
- "Then they cried out to the LORD in their trouble, and he delivered them from their distress" (vv. 6, 13, 19, 28).
- "Let them give thanks to the LORD for his unfailing love and his wonderful deeds for men" (vv. 8, 15, 21, 31).
- "He led them by a straight way to a city where they could settle" (v. 7).
- "There he brought the hungry to live, and they founded a city where they could settle" (v. 36).
- "Whoever is wise, let him heed these things and consider the great love of the LORD" (v. 43).

Also read Revelation 21:1–4.

Spiritual Formation and Urban Ministry—Opposites Repel

People who are drawn naturally to city ministry are usually action-oriented. They like to see a need and meet it. They like to see a problem and fix it. They often like to start doing something and figure they will learn by trial and error along the way.

People who are drawn naturally to spiritual formation tend to be reflection-oriented. They like to read great devotional writings of the past centuries. They can sit for long periods of time in prayer and meditation. They realize that, as they explore the depths of their own motives, they find new areas of their soul that they can surrender to God.

Amazingly, the best spiritual growth for both types of people occurs when they hang out with each other and learn from each other's natural wiring and direction. God has wired us differently like members of a body, but also connects us so that our strengths complement each others' weaknesses. Yet it is uncomfortable to enter into a place where someone's natural strength makes us feel inferior. It is easy to avoid those who are unlike us even though we know they will add so much to our spiritual growth.

As this book is a spiritual formation guide for urban ministers, and an urban ministry guide for spiritual formers, it may feel like too much inner work and motive-searching for action-oriented people. For reflective people, it may seem short and shallow. You may decide it is a tool that works best if you go through it with a group of people on the opposite side of your own gifts, temperament, and wiring.

City as a Place of Blessing, Not Merely the Place of Problems

There are two chapters at the very beginning of the Bible that demonstrate what our world was like with God as the absolute King. These chapters occur in a Garden called *Eden*. Then there are two chapters at the very end of the Bible that demonstrate what our world will be like with God as absolute King. These chapters occur in a city called *the New Jerusalem*. All the chapters in-between show what happens when God—though He remains the absolute King of the universe—for a period of time, purposefully loans a measure of His power to less-powerful creatures who are unholy.

God does not see cities as a curse. Psalm 107 demonstrates the city as a place where God gathers His people in order to bless them. Revelation 21:23 and 22:5 say that God will dwell in a city with us for eternity. Heaven is actually a city, brought down to earth. It is the perfect place for us to live for eternity. When every person is following the same leader, living in close quarters is a delight, not a pain. We are made by God to be city dwellers and we will have that blessing for eternity.

But in today's cities, every person is doing what is right in their own eyes. God who is holy, perfect, all powerful, and infinitely good is allowing others, for a time, to call the shots. Yet, amazingly, even in a high-density area of fallen humans all in rebellion against God, we can find a pungent taste of the garden and the New Jerusalem.

A Part of My Story in the City

In the mid-1980s, a friend of mine was in a Bible study and became convicted he was a slumlord. He decided that one way to alleviate this was to dedicate one of his houses to become a discipleship house for seminary students, staff, and faculty to live in and make a difference in the neighborhood that surrounded it. I was working at a seminary at that time. He knew that I lived and ministered in rough neighborhoods and asked me to help. I agreed to live at the house, recruit people to the house, and to watch over the project.

I remember the first time I saw the shell of the two-story house near Garrett Park in Dallas. All the windows were broken. The yard was hard-packed dirt and glass shards. The doors were smashed in and the inside looked like a barn with huge gaps in the floor, walls, and roof, shredded mattresses, and piles of trash. The house reeked of urine. Hypodermic needles lay in piles in several corners. The house was surrounded by three apartment complexes that had been used as crack-cocaine houses for years. We would be the first legal occupants of that part of the block in more than eight years.

Quickly the landlord's work crews put plywood over holes in the walls and slapped down uneven linoleum over gaps in the floor. They found old gas stoves and spare sinks and bolted them to the walls. They put in glass windows only to discover them all broken the next day. So they replaced them with plastic windows that the rocks would bounce off. They ladled on thick coats of paint to cover up urine stains and before long, it was ready for us to move in.

On my moving day, I dropped off a load of tools that I was going to use to install some bars over the downstairs window. When I returned with the bars, two police cars were in the yard. A plastic window was bashed in and all my tools were gone. We were what the police called a "beachhead" in the neighborhood and they had asked us to tell them the hour and day I was planning to move. They scolded me for arriving earlier than I had told them. They remained on the property as I installed the bars and moved in more things. When they left at night, I was alone in the back house.

There were yells and screeching cars all night. About 11 P.M., I heard gunfire that had that staccato sound when bullets are not aimed into the air. The police drove by, constantly flashing their lights and parking in our parking lot, but remained in their cars. A helicopter hovered overhead and shined a bright spotlight in my windows about 3 A.M. I had lived in bad places before, but this was *really* intense. I was very glad the next day when some other seminary students moved into units in the main house. Before long, we had a house of eight seminary students and staff. The local drug pushers called us "padres" even though we didn't wear clerical collars. We were "religious," which to them meant not cops and not rivals.

Two years earlier, I had bought a used truck that I was proud of owning. The first week, one of my windows was smashed and the stereo stolen. The broken steering column showed me that the hidden kill-switch I had installed on the truck kept it from driving off. I got used to not having a stereo in my truck. After the third attempt others made at stealing my car, I simply left duct tape where the window was supposed to be. We constantly found shell casings and the flat mushroom-shaped bullets that landed in our parking lot. One time at the nearby coin laundry, I saw three people shoot an Uzi machine gun into the air about 30 feet away. Everyone scurried into the laundry to avoid the falling bullets as if it were as normal as coming inside during a thunderstorm.

One day I came home and someone had attempted to use a hacksaw on my burglar bars but had given up halfway through their work. Another day I got home and someone had bashed in my front door, but the police had arrived and released a German Shepherd with muddy paws into my apartment. They told me they had caught the person hiding in my attic, terrified by the dog. It took me two days to clean up all the mud. I was really glad that the person had gotten into the attic ahead of the dog.

Living and Dying in the War Zone

The abandoned apartments in the lots behind us and on either side had become crack houses, which made this particular block a virtual war zone. Some community activists were able to use our beachhead to force the demolition of the three abandoned apartment complexes that surrounded us. One day I got home from work and the apartment complex behind me was a pile of rubble. Three days later it was an empty lot. The same happened to the two other apartment buildings in the next three months. Nine months after I arrived, I realized the night was amazingly quiet and the attempted break-ins suddenly stopped. I installed a new window and another stereo in my truck. Life was "normal" again.

The empty lots quickly became the social centers of our neighborhood. When resources are very limited, sometimes people place the greatest aspirations of their heart in their children and in their cars. Most Saturday mornings were taken up by a children's ministry to local children. Some fathers and mothers would often sit through the whole program, singing children's songs (but never making the silly motions). I was surprised how the urban code allowed even the toughest teenagers to soften their faces for almost an hour *if* they were helping a younger sibling learn how to "be good."

On Saturday afternoons, men would gather in the field behind our house, pull a car into the lot, jack it up, take off a tire, and open the hood. The rest of the day they sat drinking beer and telling stories. Occasionally a woman would yell at them from a nearby apartment balcony and they would take off the air cleaner cover to make it appear even more as if they were working on the car. When I sat with them, they were happy to have someone new to whom they could tell their well-worn stories. We eventually figured out a way to string an extension cord to a small TV that was blocked by an electrical switch box so it couldn't be seen from the balconies as we watched weekend sports.

One Saturday morning, I woke up to perhaps the strangest scene yet. In our parking lot and alongside the street were parked more than 10 sparkling BMW's, Mercedes, and Cadillacs. A group of women in brightly colored dresses with perfectly matching high heels were picking their way through our yard. The Junior League had arrived to survey the site of the big Habitat for Humanity build-out. The beachhead had been established. It was now time for the suburban teams to arrive every Saturday to build new houses on our block. Over the next several years, they would build 37 simple homes on and near our street.

For the next two years the suburban work crews came down each Saturday. For most, it was something they did as part of a missions team. Some would make comments about "the great sacrifice *I* was making to live 'down here.'" Some seemed nervous. Some seemed more at home than I did. Some teams arrived late and left early. Other teams arrived early and worshiped together for 30 minutes before the supplies arrived and stayed 30 minutes afterward, reflecting on how they saw Jesus in the people and events of the day.

However, a few people starting hanging out during the week and evenings. One older man said his suburban neighborhood didn't have any porches anymore. He asked if he could borrow ours. He said it made him feel like the neighborhood he grew up with—everyone out on the street talking to each other. Others came over and spent a great deal of extra time adding special cabinets, planting bushes, and just fussing over the new Habitat houses. It was almost as if something had captured their heart in ways that made it impossible for them to see it as merely a weekend project. Since churches adopted individual houses, some stayed after their house was finished to help us with the local children's ministry and sit with the parents as they listened to us tell Bible stories to the children.

One night, a random drive-by shooting hit a four-year-old boy sleeping innocently in the front bedroom of a Habitat house across from our front porch. The bullet lodged just above the roof of his mouth. People in both the Garrett Park neighborhood and our sister neighborhoods in the suburbs rallied to help the family as the boy went through a difficult surgery. We had all seen so many impossible situations, but somehow this one was so unfair that all we could do was cry and express the futility of life in our neighborhood. Eventually we learned the boy would survive without brain damage. Several people remarked at how they found it amazing that we didn't have to cover up our feelings of despair.

One man sitting on the porch remarked, "This time last week year I was busy worrying about my church committees and the golf tournament at the country club. Thank you for providing a place where I can worry about caring for real people and real needs."

Another remarked, "I am so burned-out on church work and programs. This Habitat project allowed me to get off all those committees and reenter the real world of relationships. I feel more like I'm worshipping God nailing drywall here than I ever did in our beautiful sanctuary with the full orchestra and choir."

A few actually moved to the neighborhood. Some moved from very nice homes in the suburbs. They talked about how great it was to be able to *walk* to the grocery store with friends. They liked spending evenings on the street curbs rather than inside watching TV. The longer they lived nearby, the more they talked about how the big plastic malls made them feel dizzy and how the eight-foot-high yard fences they used to have in the suburbs were making less and less sense to them.

Home Away from Home

My own journey in this neighborhood was one from discomfort to comfort, then discomfort again. At first I was intimidated by Garrett Park. It was far more intense than the previous "bad neighborhoods" where I had lived. Later, as I started making new friends, it began to feel like home—a place where I had lived much longer than what the calendar said. People trusted me as a leader. I was able to provide resources they had not had before. Because of our Saturday children's ministry, it was hard to walk very far without being stopped by a child who wanted a hug or to share something with the excitement that only an eight-year-old can express. I don't think I've ever seen so many smiling, hopeful, beautiful children in one neighborhood before that time, or since. At the grocery store, laundry, local restaurants—everywhere I went there were friends, conversations, stories, laughter, and a chance to be the neighborhood pastor. People in the neighborhood acted like they wanted me to make decisions for them. Some were very appreciative of all the new resources and help that was pouring into our streets. My feelings changed from intimidation to a sense that this was my home.

For the most part, I experienced what the Bible says is joy. I think *joy* can be defined as peace in any circumstance, based on trust in God's character. Some days, I experienced happiness too. Yet there were many health, relationship, medical, and injustice tragedies that were taking place throughout our neighborhood and many days were sad and frustrating.

Much of what I did in Garrett Park came from a genuine sense of love of people and an enjoyment in serving others. Yet, I also began to experience something else—a mixed motive. In a ridiculously short amount of time, I became proud of what I did and where I lived. It made me feel significant. When I was outside of the neighborhood, it gave me a unique identity. In 1988, the seminary decided to focus on our work as the main theme of their fundraising campaign. They filmed us with the children. They filmed the trash in abandoned lots and interviewed us. They asked us to speak at banquets. What before was mostly non-eventful daily life suddenly became exciting and heroic in the sound-bite world.

Yet after the rush of publicity, I started feeling very strange about being in the neighborhood. My mentors had taught me to recruit teams of residents to interface with nonprofit agencies and governmental entities. They told me these residents knew much more about what was needed than I did and that, over time, I would become more in the way than helpful. What they didn't tell me was how addicted I would get to always having to be the hero and how empty it felt to be deadwood in meetings where I formerly was the star.

Often on Saturday nights, we'd sit on the porch and laugh about what we had seen from the "weekenders" that day. There are always a few people from the suburbs who do and say funny things when they first come to a "bad neighborhood." It was easy for us to judge the motives of these "one-day urban warriors" who'd come down, paint a little, get some pictures with our friends, and then leave, smug in their generosity.

One Saturday night as we sat around laughing about things we saw that day, it suddenly dawned on me that I was the only person on the porch who had the financial means to pack up and leave if I wanted to do so. No matter how accepted I was, it still made me an outsider—just another kind of weekender. I just listened that night. It hit me like a kick in the face. As I listened to the banter, I realized in a way, they were talking about me too. While there were many good motives in my heart, I was also a "user" in good Samaritan clothing. I began to wonder, "Why do I *really* live here?"

Weekenders often wore their insecurities on their sleeves and acted them out in fearful or even condescending ways. I also had deep insecurities, but the longer I lived in the neighborhood, and the more I became the neighborhood leader and pastor, the easier it was for me to hide these fears from myself and others. In a way, that made me much more dangerous to the people I loved in the neighborhood than the weekenders were.

I met with some of the other seminary students in our Discipleship House and slowly began to share how I suspected my mixed motives. Unfortunately, some of them took this all too seriously and decided they would help me on my journey toward finding more of my heart motives. They told me in very astute ways that they saw my motives as far more ugly than what I had allowed myself to see. What I saw in the mirror they provided was hideous. My little venture into false humility was becoming truly humiliating.

Caution: Brokenness Ahead

We kept talking. Each of us has motives this side of heaven that are complex mixtures of good and bad. Urban community living has a way of putting a much-needed spotlight on both the good and the bad inside us. We all dared to ask the hard question of "Why are we *really* here?"

Some felt they were failures in the suburban social climbing wars and wanted away from the pressure. Others realized they liked the superior feeling of living among people with less money and less education, who needed them. Some of us had self-images shaped by years of legalistic shame or, in some cases, even abusive families. We found that the more ugly the place we lived and the more meanly we were treated, the more it confirmed a misfit self-image with which we were comfortable.

Some of us were facing embarrassing and public crises in our lives and were tired of the strange questions from people searching for the cause. We felt as though they wanted to comfort themselves that their legalistic behavior could keep a similar circumstance from entering their lives. Our self-exile to the ghetto kept these pain-avoiding "formula" Christians away from us. Others in our group realized they had deep pain but were cursed with "Anglo suburban emotional autism" which limited their ability to express pain. They came to the neighborhood to live vicariously through the rich emotional expressiveness of black and brown brothers and sisters—leeching off others' freedom to express their pain. Others liked the way their urban lifestyle made them look cool among suburban friends.

My day job during this period was leading the spiritual formation program at a nearby seminary. Intellectually, we understood that the antithesis of spiritual formation was attempting to make our lives work apart from God. The beginning of spiritual formation is a brokenness of heart, emotions, plans, and strategies so that we would find our only hope in dependence on God. Healthy spiritual formation is like looking through a telescope in one eye to see the character of God, and through a microscope in the other eye to see our own sinful hearts and how our sin contributes to our cynicism about God's character. Over time, our hope in God's character increases as we become less impressed with our own efforts to be godly. Brokenness is a vital part of this journey.

I had lectured on brokenness for years. I had had severe circumstances in my life that had been far more painful than living in a ghetto that I had assumed would automatically lead me to brokenness. I had shared cleanly-edited personal illustrations in the classroom and sermons. I thought I was being so authentic and deep. Yet, as I watched my own ugly and evil motives being revealed, I realized that I was clueless about brokenness.

The definition for what it means to be *broken* before God is still intensely confusing to me. It is something I know is real when I see it in others or feel it in myself. But it is something that is ridiculous to define and certainly impossible to call up at will.

Yet there is something about urban ministry, when done in honest community, which can help brokenness enter into our lives. And in spite of what every rational thought in us says to the contrary, brokenness is something we really, really want to be part of our daily experience as much as possible.

During this time, for me there was a convergence of many circumstances, good and evil people, good and bad advice, and mostly accidental choices that felt like a 2-by-4 across my face to drive me to the ground in abject surrender before God. I felt like I had two coils of thick, scratchy rope wound tightly around me. The rope that was a result of my own motives and choices was scary. Yet, amazingly, the other rope that felt it was put there by the hand of God was very comforting. I wanted my ropes off, and God's ropes to remain. Surprisingly, I found myself wanting God to limit my freedom, limit my options, limit my rights, limit my success. For the first time, I really trusted the limits He placed in my life. I needed brokenness to get my own fat head out of the way so I could see the delight of God's eyes in me as His creature, who did absolutely nothing in my own strength to earn His gleam of delight.

The Book of Job, some of the laments of David in the Psalms, and much of the prophetic books in the Old Testament describe in rich detail the work of God to bring us to the reality of true brokenness through tough circumstances, honest friends, and severe futility. I was thankful that I had some really severe circumstances combined with some really honest friends to push my face into the realities I was scrambling to avoid.

Yet even severe circumstances, both before and since that time, have never been a sure thing to create authentic brokenness in my heart. In most cases, the more severe the circumstances, the more frantically I scramble to "turn lemons into lemonade"; "to find the pony hidden in the manure pile"; or to "hunker down and outwork the pain." I can always find a very confident group of religious friends who will help me disassociate into an unreal world of spiritual language, false positives, or publicly approved addictive behaviors such as workaholism—all designed to keep the brokenness at bay.

In part, I moved to the urban setting to be where I could be the hero; people would need me and appreciate me and I could make a life that would work for me apart from God. In part I moved to the neighborhood because somewhere deep inside I knew I needed to be broken and surrendered before God. My theory was that I would be most able to be dependent upon God if I were the most unable to control the circumstances surrounding me. It wasn't a bad theory. It might be written in a formula like this:

bad circumstances = brokenness ➝ *leads to* ➝ spiritual formation

No, it is not a bad formula. But it is not a complete formula. I learned that the formula also needs *honest relationships* somewhere in the mix. And honest relationships are much harder to find than bad circumstances.

Green Light: Honest Thoughts and Emotions

For most of us, deep honesty rarely comes from individual reflection, intense spiritual discipline, or even massive amounts of religious activity. I am skeptical of deep, honest, one-way communication because it is so controlled by the speaker, and so easy to wrap up by the end of the sermon. And I know how often I use one-way communication of my "deep" brokenness to distract myself and others so I don't have to experience real brokenness. My rule of thumb for myself is that if I am in control of the deep sharing of my heart, then it probably isn't real. In my life, people who have well-developed Crap-O-Meters and aren't afraid to use them in a loving way on me are worth their weight in gold.

The spiritual formation program I was leading at the seminary involved almost 600 students. The best part was that we had to be *in* an honest group in order *to lead* an honest group. I had many people speaking hard, truthful things into my life. Since the leaders were both men and women, one of my personal groups was a mixed-gender group. There I learned that women could lead many of us emotionally autistic men past our elaborate intellectual explanations to a deeper emotional place where we had to cry "Uncle!" before each other and God.

But most of our groups were single-gender groups only. So I found a four-page list of "emotion words" from a counselor and copied it for all the men-only groups. It was like we had discovered a lost civilization. We were amazed at how many words the English language has for emotions. We had to look up most of the words in the dictionary because we had heard our mothers, sisters, girlfriends, or wives use them, but we had never bothered to figure out what these words actually meant. As ridiculous as this scene would have looked if we had ever allowed a women to see it (and we did not), as we shared with each other, we pulled out our list of emotion words and coaxed each other to go through the list to find a word that stated most accurately what we felt. It was a formulaic and weird method, but it did actually work.

We found the emotion-word pages actually helped us talk more honestly about the hidden forces inside that could unlock the mysteries of brokenness before God. It changed the depth of our prayers, how we understood the same words in Scripture, and how we preached. And not surprisingly, I had wife after wife of men in these groups who approached me telling me how our groups were making their husbands more expressive. We never told our secret of our emotion-word cheat sheets, but I know a few friends who, to this day, carry them and use them daily like a foreign language pocket translator.

So I had to update my "formula for spiritual growth" to something like:

Bad circumstance + honest friends = brokenness ➙ *leads to* ➙ greater dependence upon God ➙ *which is the key to* ➙ spiritual formation

Of course I live as a Christian in a subculture obsessed with finding *the formula* to control God to make our lives work well, so about the time this formula for spiritual formation makes sense, it would be wise to trash it. God is fairly serious about not letting us control Himself, and He is ultimately the One to form us spiritually. However, the formula helped me capture my learning at that point in my life.

Because of this, for me, the story of urban ministry is also a story of deep, honest, confusing, and often painful relationships that I could not control. Ministry and relationships have to go together. In the urban setting among people of different cultures, I learned that my attempts to make my life work apart from God appeared very foolish to those who were not caught up in my particular style of the same rat race. As far as those of us in the Discipleship House, we realized that every one of us had come to the neighborhood largely for selfish motives, masquerading them as something selfless. But somehow the urban landscape, the added conflicts of being in close proximity to each other, the frank questions of the locals who could smell our attitudes of superiority, and the extra time spent on the porches had made us all the more human. We were less impressed with ourselves, and on a few particularly good days, more in love with this place and the people that had saved us from living the plastic, hidden lives that money and privilege offered as an option.

We realized that most of us originally saw the city as a place of so many problems that we were unable to see it as a place of so many blessings. It was a place to visit and fix. It was a place to use to validate our personal sense of significance. We thought we had come to this ugly, broken place to be sound-bite heroes. Instead, we met heroes who already lived there and they became a blessing to us. It is the great irony of life in the city.

Red Lights: Stop to See the Substance

By the early 1990s, they tore down our house on the corner because it didn't meet the standards of a Habitat for Humanity neighborhood and replaced it with a Habitat home. I moved to plant and pastor a church in another "bad neighborhood" nearby, even closer to downtown. Today, the Garrett Park neighborhood has stylish urban condos right next to our Habitat homes. Not too far away are brand-new buildings built to look like old warehouses. They are full of expensive lofts—built to look old but with the latest commercial kitchens and electrical gadgets. There are upscale markets and food shops nearby; stylish restaurants mixed in with the original pool hall dives; and old bars that look the same as they always did. The city is being regentrified. My former neighbors are being forced to move to the first ring of suburbs just outside the first freeway loop that encircles our city. Their bus rides to work are now at least 30 minutes longer. They are in broken-down apartment complexes built in the 1970s rather than the 1940s. They have to work much harder to find the natural community spaces they left behind.

Urban has now become chic. In the 1960s and 1970s, Hollywood communicated idealism through suburban-based sitcoms such as *The Brady Bunch* and *Happy Days*. A dominant style of dress was the suburban inspired "preppie." Today, the sitcoms and feature movies that spotlight people with "exciting lives" are largely set in urban settings. In contrast, movies such as *American Beauty*, *The Stepford Wives*, and sitcoms, including *Desperate Housewives*, and others set in suburban settings often portray that life as boring and severely dysfunctional. At an urban clothing store you can buy ultra-chic clothes copying designs birthed in the 'hood. Suburban school students mimic the walk, dress, speech, and music styles of inner-city gangs. What used to be slums are now ultra-chic urban-styled malls.

It doesn't mean that poverty, prejudice, injustice, inequality, pain, crime, disease, drugs, violence, and alienation have been solved. All it means is that, in some cases, these have been dispersed from former urban pockets to new ones in different locations. In most cases, it means these same old problems are hidden better behind a new community center, an urban strip mall, or an economic zone that distracts attention from the massive problems a few streets beyond them.

For those of us in urban ministry, we realize that the world has suddenly learned of the beauty of the city. People are attracted to the diversity, community, and texture of the city. Yet, while they may have found the beauty, in most cases they are missing the substance of what makes the city truly beautiful. Brokenness before God is the true treasure that the city can bring if a person is pursuing it. But the same people who in the first generation moved to the suburbs to escape the pain of being too close to their neighbor are now moving back to the city in the second generation to escape the pain of isolation. Escaping pain is rarely in any formula for genuine brokenness. And as I look at the pristine condos with warehouse-like exteriors, it seems like we are attempting to re-make a new city with false promises of only green lights. But it is the red lights—where we must stop and experience our and others' need of the King—that create the great strength of the city.

▪ ▪ ▪ Personal Reflection

Most of us go to the city at first simply to help people, make some new friends, and maybe make a small difference in someone's life. Just getting involved and seeing what happens is the best way to open our hearts to what God wants to teach us.

Yet not long into our urban ministry journey, we experience both intense joy and frustration. These intense experiences in the midst of reflection and relationships can facilitate a parallel spiritual formation journey that opens up whole new ways to reflect on God and His work in our lives.

The best place to start on this second parallel journey is exploring God's presence in your own story. There is an art and a unique love in telling your story in a way that releases someone else's deeper story. Your story is given to you by God. In building relationships in the city, your story is a treasure more valuable than any expertise, time, or money you bring.

The high points of your story (your successes) may impress people, but the hard times (your failures) are what inspire their trust in you. It takes much practice to share the pain of your life authentically without hiding behind stoicism or over-dramatization. There is much about spiritual formation that seems contrary to logic. There is much about urban ministry that empowers the poor, rather than just meets a need, that also seems contrary to logic. An often repeated saying among urban ministry veterans is, "If you are going to start with need, start with your own." I'll explain that in more detail later, but at this point it is important to start by learning to share the part of your story that shows you have needs too.

Urban ministry that leads to spiritual growth always involves ever-deepening relationships with people like you, not like you, and even people who don't like you. So, as you prepare to move deeper into urban ministry—and hopefully toward brokenness before God—the best starting place is your own story. As you tell your story, include:

Your passion:

Each of us has a story of how we've become drawn to the city. What has made you consider urban ministry as part of your personal call?

What has caused the city to be a place that you increasingly call home in spite of all the things you experience there that are painful and frustrating?

Why do you find your energy increase and your senses sharpen the more you live, develop relationships, and minister in the city?

Your pain:

What have been the hardest times in your life?

Where have you failed or found yourself just confused?

What is one time of your life that you wish you could have fast-forwarded through or avoided?

As you think about your life right now, what do you find as something you fear?

Something you wish would change?

Something that you worry about and perhaps even cry about?

Your heart:

Why are you involved in *urban ministry?*

Look at the following reasons why people minister in the city—both the good reasons and the not-so-good. Which two or three ring most true to you?

(1) I grew up in the city. This is my home; these are my family and friends. Urban ministry is what God gave me as my life.

(2) I grew up in many kinds of poverty, but God graciously delivered me. Now I am back among the poor because I know their hearts. I want them to experience the hope I have found.

(3) I didn't grow up in the heart of the city, but now urban ministry is where I feel at home. I fit here. It is where I most experience true worship of God.

(4) When I minister in the city, I feel needed. My ideas are respected. I enjoy the sense of being important and useful.

(5) Urban ministry gives me a style, a unique story, and a way to be set apart from everyone else.

(6) I minister in the city because that is what God commands. It is often not enjoyable or comfortable, but it is my calling.

(7) In urban ministry, my work has concrete and immediate results in people's lives. I like the practicality of helping people overcome obstacles in measurable ways.

(8) Urban ministry is a fascinating learning experience. I love meeting and knowing many diverse people. I minister in the city because it is interesting and full of new experiences.

(9) I minister in the city because I am selfish and God is using this work to open up my heart to love in deeper ways. My spirit is impoverished and I find my relationships with people who are financially impoverished bring riches to my heart.

(10) I minister in the city, but to the powerful. My call is to change systems of injustice. God has given me a position of influence that I want to use to benefit the vulnerable. I also have a calling to my peers. I am in the city to give true hope to those who are addicted to the false gods of power, fame, and wealth.

(11) I don't know why the city is such a magnet for me. I hope to learn more through this study.

(12) I'm not really involved in the city but am curious about it. I hope to see through this study if this is something that piques my interest.

Recognizing we all have mixed motives this side of heaven, how would you answer your reasons for focusing on city ministry? Take a moment to write a paragraph or two about your reasons for being involved in the city using a few of the 12 reasons above as a beginning place for your thoughts. It is hoped that over the course of this study, you will be able to answer this question with new clarity and understanding of your call.

■ ■ ■ Bible Reflection

Read Psalm 107.
When have you experienced times of wilderness, chains, rebellion, or tempest?

When have you experienced times of being safe, settled, and fruitful?

How did you experience God during both times of trouble and times of blessing?

How has the city or cross-cultural experiences/relationships contributed to both pain and joy in your life?

How do you hope this study will help you experience:

Brokenness: "cry out to the Lord in your trouble,"

Gratitude: "thank God for his unfailing love and wonderful deeds," and

Worship: "consider the great love of the Lord" (Psalm 107)?

How do you hope this study will help you see a bigger God than you now know?

Chapter Two: BIG WORLD, BIG GOD

The Cities Reveal the Nations—The Nations Reveal God

Spiritual Formation Principle #2: The turmoil of the fast-changing global urban landscape opens us to have a bigger view of God.

Theme: The nations are in motion to the city. The global cities reveal the nations and the nations reveal God. God has called us to witness to the nations. Today that calling can be part of our everyday life more than ever before.

Bible Reading:
Matthew 28:18–20
Acts 1:7–8
Romans 16:25–27
Revelation 7:9–10

A World in Motion

The greatest force of change in urban ministry in the last 15 years has come from changes in the demography of the city. At the end of chapter one, if you shared an urban ministry story from the decade of the 1980s with your group, it might have had similar themes to mine. Years ago, urban ministry was mostly about the "inner city"—a neighborhood close to downtown. It most likely was a story about social services, such as providing housing, food, clothing, medical care, or education. It may have involved people with white, black, or brown skin, all of whose parents were from North or Central America.

However, if you chose a story from the decades of the 1990s or later, it is more likely that the neighborhood was further out from downtown since many downtown housing projects in the US were bulldozed in that decade. Your story might involve more occasions of putting on a suit and meeting with city officials, or writing business plans or grant requests. We'll discuss more of these trends later.

What you might especially notice in the more recent stories of urban ministry is that the groups involved have been more likely not only Americans, but also Asians, Africans, Eastern Europeans, Middle Easterners, and others. And the location of the stories has been increasingly outside of North America. More and more urban ministry tasks involve working with Immigration and Naturalization Services (INS) officials and visa offices to reunite families; teaching English to many language groups beyond Spanish; and sometimes even relating to family members who are in frequent migration between continents.

Large cities are the hubs of tumultuous worldwide migration streams. The center of the church has been moving beyond North America.

The Continents Are Reconnecting

Before my first trip to Russia in 1994, I was given a list about how not to be a conspicuous American. One item on the list read, "Do not wear American sports team T-shirts." I recall later sitting on a Moscow subway, counting 17 American sports team T-shirts on the Russian young people in that one car alone. I was almost conspicuous for *not* wearing one.

Twelve years later, wearing a Houston Rockets Yao Ming jersey on the streets of Beijing, I was treated as if I were walking down the street holding high the Chinese national flag. Often youth on the street grinned or even stopped to express in excited Chinese their shared love for Yao Ming. Teams and international brands create immediate fraternities of people who have never met, have huge cultural barriers between them, and don't even speak the same language.

Last year I was with 550 young leaders aged 25 to 35, carefully selected from around the world, to attend a networking conference. These leaders were broken into small groups, most of which had at least four continents represented in the group. I listened to story after story of how they had been so much more exposed to the West through the Internet, Hollywood, and local business opportunities in their city that they found themselves not just a generation away, but a world away from their parents and many aspects of their native culture. One person from Bangalore, India, remarked that his job in a call center gave him more money in one year than his father, grandfather, great-grandfather, and great-great-grandfather combined had made in their whole lives. He told me it was very hard for his parents to understand the opportunities and cultural changes brought by globalization, but now that he had tasted these, he could never go back to their world. He felt both exhilarated and profoundly lonely.

Yet, every one of these leaders also did not want to become either Americanized—or so completely Western-influenced—that they would lose their roots. They felt lost between their home culture where they no longer belonged and a Western culture that they no longer wanted to mimic. They remarked that the place they felt most connected was with other young leaders, even from other cultures, who were in the same place—lost between cultures. I call this phenomenon the "Global Youth Diaspora." It is a growing global community of urban-dwelling, English-speaking youth connected by online tools such as MySpace, Yahoo Groups, YouTube, and Skype, sharing a common journey. Connection between people of different continents that used to take years of language struggles, social faux pas, and agonizing trust-building can happen in mere weeks in this global youth Diaspora. Churches in the US, who send youth groups on short-term mission trips to urban centers, often remark at how fast they connect with the youth of the city they visited.

Global movements of connection and migration are happening through the gateways of global cities. We can't even imagine how they will change our world in the next two decades.

The Nations Are in Motion to the City

In 1900, 90 percent of US residents lived in rural regions. Today, 90 percent of the US lives in urban regions. In China, almost 30 million people are moving from rural regions to cities each year. That is the equivalent of the whole population of Canada getting into moving vans each year. The US has 10 cities with more than a million people. China already has 180 cities with more than a million people and is building about 10 new cities each year to handle the massive population migration. According to www.citymayors.com projections, by 2020, the five largest cities in the world will be:

Tokyo, Japan	37.3 million
Mumbai, India	26.1 million
Delhi, India	25.8 million
Dhaka, Bangladesh	22.0 million
Mexico City, Mexico	21.8 million

Demographic experts tell us that in 2007, for the first time in recorded human history (since the tower of Babel), more humans in the world lived in an urban regions rather than in rural regions. We have crossed the threshold of history that started in a rural garden in the first two chapters of Genesis and will end in a city in the last two chapters of Revelation.

Yet the migration streams are not only from rural-to-urban within countries, but also urban-to-urban between continents. UN statistics show unprecedented migrant streams from Africa to Europe, from Asia to North America and Australia, and from South America to North America. In addition to migrants, there are also vast guest worker, expatriate, and undocumented-worker temporary workforce flows. An estimated one million Filipino guest-workers travel to the Middle East, Asia, Europe, Australia, and the Americas each year. The US has close to three million expatriates living overseas.

Six decades ago, international air travel was only for the very wealthy or the military. The airline statistics company, OAG, calculated that the world's airlines offered a record 3.3 billion seats on 28.2 million flights during 2006. That represents an average daily offer of more than nine million seats on 77,371 individual daily flights. Never has the world been in so much motion!

In the US, the urban migration over 100 years has drastically changed US society. Even more so, in places such as China, India, and Africa, people are moving from villages that have ancestral roots, beliefs, and traditions that have remained largely unchanged for several hundred years. The city turns these belief systems upside-down and opens them up for whole new ways—either for good or for bad. Never has the world been so open to new ideas and new faiths.

In 2001, 30 percent of the world's population was between 15 and 24 years old. Eighty-three percent of the people under the age of 25 were living in the developing world. In India, more than 500 million people were less than 25 years old, and with a population growth rate of almost 1.4 percent, India has been projected to be the world's most populous nation by 2025. In an age of technology and growing capital markets, those who are young migrate faster and connect cross-culturally much more easily than those who are older. Never before has the world been so young and in such transition to new lifestyles.

In the first decade of the second millenium, one billion people have become users of the Internet. Theoretically, you could reach 15 percent of the world's population with a keystroke on your home computer. Cable Network News (CNN) became a 24-hour, worldwide news network, allowing much of the world's population to hear news from any place in the world in mere moments after it has happened. Never before in the history of the world has such a large number and such a large percentage of the world's population been so easily connected.

Today, more than 40 percent of the world population lives in two countries, India and China. In contrast, only 5 percent of the world's population lives in North America. Prior to 1990, two great superpowers in the world were in a tug of war over political ideology. Most countries were labeled in the media and journals as aligning themselves either with democracy or communism and we heard terms like "The Iron Curtain" or "The Bamboo Curtain." In 1991, the Soviet Union dissolved and, almost overnight, nations were no longer defined by political ideologies. Instead, they are labeled as *developed*, *developing*, or *not developed;* defined by how well they are accessing the international capitalist markets. For the first time in almost 1,000 years, the world is no longer centered around European and US conflicts, alliances, and colonial endeavors. The center of the world is fast becoming more about multinational companies and economic connections, especially in Asia.

China has accessed this new world so well that it has sustained the world's fastest economic growth rate—9 percent per year for at least four years—in history. If you are older than 50, think about how quickly the term *The Bamboo Curtain* disappeared from our language. What used to be closed off and mysterious 20 years ago has become a favorite tourist, business, and media destination.

India is often called the "back office of the world" as it connects to the world through customer service call centers and myriad outsourcing industries. With an estimated 300 million English speakers, India is now the largest English-speaking nation in the world.

Because of the Internet, Hollywood, and Wall Street, English also has become the international business language. In South Korea, there is a widespread surgical procedure among youth to clip the frenulum—a small connecting tissue beneath the tongue, to allow better pronunciation of English *l* and *r* sounds. Without iron and bamboo curtains, with the widespread use of English, and with the growth of international free markets, never before has so much of the world been so accessible to English-speaking people.

As a result of all of these tectonic changes in our world, most major cities are fast becoming microcosms of the whole world.

Most likely, in your city there is a geographical section where recent immigrants from China live, and another section for immigrants from Thailand, or Vietnam, or South Korea, or Nigeria, or Ethiopia. In addition to these local neighborhood-based re-creations of the nations, there are also vast but invisible cultural networks. All you have to do is develop a relationship with one well-connected Ugandan who has lived in your city for at least four or five years and, suddenly, a whole new map is opened up to you that shows a well-connected network of Ugandans throughout your city. On top of this invisible map of recent immigrants are other networks of Ugandan professionals, small business owners, and students who are on short-term assignments in the city, but who remain integrally connected to their home cultures. Never before has the whole world been so near to your doorstep!

The gateway to engaging this newly connected and accessible world is your own city. If we mapped the world by social-economic and communication connections rather than by nationality, we would be amazed. In most developing countries, the differences between city-dwellers and rural-dwellers in the same country is many times more pronounced than the difference between those same city-dwellers and their counterparts across an ocean. People in New York have more connections and more similarities of lifestyle with people in Shanghai than the people in Shanghai have with people in their own nation, who live 30 miles away in a rural village. When we engage our own city, we have opened a door to engage the world.

The City Reveals the Nations and the Nations Reveal God

You may have noticed from chapter one and your or your group's stories after chapter one that much of what people enjoy about urban ministry is the way it forces us away from our own comfort zones, makes us think about the needs of others more than our own needs, and builds relationships with people who speak into our lives in fresh ways. For most, urban ministry is a journey of personal/community discipleship and spiritual formation. The key to its power is that it forces us away from what we understand and can control into a place of confusion and inadequacy. It is in the place of inadequacy that we are most open to see our profound dependence on God. And, the recognition of God's amazing goodness and power and our profound dependence upon God is the tap root of spiritual formation.

This sense of inadequacy is even greater as barriers of language, culture, and worldview grow larger. As migration streams increase the cultural diversity of the city, the work of urban ministry becomes increasingly complex.

If self-sufficiency and feelings of success in our attempts to make our lives work apart from God is the antidote to spiritual formation, then inadequacy, confusion, and frustration brought to us by the complexity of urban ministry can lead us to a full dose of trust and dependency on God. Trust and dependency on God is the central goal of spiritual formation. The more we are inadequate and confused, the closer we are to being formed by God. An increasingly culturally diverse and connected world can bring confusion and inadequacy to our doorstep.

Intersections of Our Weakness and God's Omnipotence

Yet there is another ingredient. For many people, spiritual formation is at its height when personal inadequacy intersects with the work of God expressed and seen in fresh new ways. It is both the exposure to personal inadequacy *and* exposure to the absolute adequacy of God that forms us. There are few spiritual formation environments more full of these two ingredients than global urban ministry— either in a local city or abroad. Bible passages that we have read 100 times take on a new meaning when we hear how people with a different cultural background apply them in their own lives. Areas of personal sin that our own culture justifies becomes glaring rebellion against God through the eyes of another culture who has different blindsides. Christian disciplines that have become rote after years of practice suddenly come alive again in a community of Christians from a different cultural background that do it completely differently.

Global Cities Disrupt Our Attempts to Minimize God

The dawning of the 21st century is a rich age for Christians who are spiritually formed in adversity, diversity, and challenge. There is a familiar story in India of four blind men who come across an elephant. The first one feels the huge stocky leg and claims that he has found a tree. The second bumps against the huge stomach and, after feeling the side of the elephant, claims he is now facing a high, rough wall. The third reaches up and touches the tail and claims that he has found a piece of rope. The fourth holds the trunk and exclaims that he is holding a large snake.

Those with sight can stand back and see the whole, but those without sight can only see the pieces and draw conclusions about the whole from the parts. In John 6:46, Jesus says, "No one has seen the Father except the one who is from God; only he has seen the Father." When it comes to seeing God, we are all blind—each of us sees a part, but no one sees the whole.

Like the blind men, we tend to reduce God to the part that we can most easily comprehend. All of us have the inclination to reduce God to someone smaller than He really is so that we can ultimately control Him. It is not always a conscious desire, but it is the natural inclination of all of us this side of heaven.

Several years ago I heard about a church nearby that was holding 5 A.M. prayer meetings attended by more than 500 people. Not wanting to miss a fresh infusion of God's power in my own life, I set my alarm for 4 A.M. and got a front row seat. Throughout the hour, the pastor encouraged us from the microphone as we prayed in groups, out loud or silently. However, his message was consistently, "If you ask fervently enough; if you make this sacrifice to get up this early; if you do this list of actions, God is *obligated* to bless you." By the end of the hour, I felt God was reduced to our butler to come at our beck and call if only we followed the right formula. It is not a surprise that the 5 A.M. prayer meetings eventually faded away as people began to realize that God wasn't fulfilling the obligations they had placed on Him.

God will not allow Himself to be placed in a bottle to grant us our wishes as though He were a genie. His ways are far above our ways and our first approach in prayer should be to acknowledge that we trust Him even if we cannot control Him. However, He answers our prayers. Even if His answers are not always what we would have chosen, those answers are the work of a God who loves us beyond what we can imagine.

True prayer and worship don't start by looking at all that we have done, what we need, and how we can convince God to give it to us. It starts by being reminded that we are the creatures and God is the Creator. No matter what we think we need, the One who created us knows our true needs and loves us so much that He will even override our requests and make us face our disappointments to give us what is best.

Like rivaling siblings, we tend to reduce God's preferences to those things that *we* are best able to meet. I recall Fred Smith Sr. saying one time that "God offers us a *personal* relationship, but what we really want is a *preferential* relationship." These messages are subtle and never this direct, but it is like the Baptist saying, "We know God loves all people of all denominations, but God especially loves those who are active in evangelism." Or the Charismatic believer saying, "God loves everyone, but the special place in His heart is for those who worship Him the most fervently." Or the Presbyterian saying, "God loves all of His people, but His favorites are those with the *right* theology." We so badly want God to fit *us*, to prefer *us*. So we picture Him as being preferential to people who are like us: those who are pastors, or those who have disciplined temperaments, or those who are wealthy, or those who are poor. Perhaps most damaging is that we picture God as agreeing with our own subtle views of the superiority of our "racial" identification, our nationality, or our culture.

So we stand like blind men before an elephant, arguing fervently that our view is right. It is not surprising that a culture like the United States that emphasizes personal freedoms sees God as a personal God. Or that a matriarchal culture sees God as a protecting mother, or that an ancient culture connected by extended families of multiple generations sees God as their connection to their cultural traditions, their ancestors, and the generations that will follow them. Perhaps some of those things are true about God, but our arguing about our view is keeping us convinced that God is a tree, wall, rope, or snake and we miss the blessing of seeing a bigger God.

Transforming Power

The power of global urban ministry for our own spiritual formation is that it is a cold splash of water in the face, waking us up to the fact that God is much, much bigger than we ever imagined. Working cross-culturally is a constant worship experience as we are continually reminded that God chooses whom to bless according to *His* logic, not ours. Any hidden formulas that we have had about how to control God are dispelled in front of our faces, over and over again. Any thought that God prefers people like us is shown to be false.

The basic truths of Christianity based in the Bible remain above any cultural expression, but they are understood and practiced in different ways. US culture is built around the idea of the self-sufficient individual always moving westward. Unlike any other culture, we have a unique understanding of the personal, individual aspects of God's saving grace as well as the real hope of a more positive future place called The New Jerusalem of Revelation 21.

On the other hand, Japan has one of the most communal cultures in the world, formed over many centuries of being an island nation in isolation from other cultures. The Japanese culture possesses unique eyes for God's community within the Trinity and in the body of Christ as one, fully connected entity. Many African Christians expect and understand the power of God to heal and transform in supernatural ways that are not squashed by a Western mind-set that demands scientific proof or develop a rational explanation.

With the world more connected and accessible to new ideas, we are for the first time seeing how God has chosen to reveal Himself for 4,000-plus years in cultures that are unlike our own. The city I live in is about 160 years old. A house I bought that was built in 1924 was designated as being in an historic district. My children spend a great deal of time in their school, studying state and national history that occurred in the 18th century. In contrast, in other cultures, the 18th century would be a mere blip in thousands of years of God's work in their cultural and national history.

For example, new evidence is emerging in China of God's work for 3,500 years to establish a culture that understands sacrificial atonement. The Altar of Heaven in Beijing was used every year since the early 15th century to sacrifice an unblemished calf to atone for the sins of the emperor and the emperor's people. This calf was being offered to a god called "the God above the Emperor"—so great that no image could be made to depict him. Another smaller altar has been found in Xian and other evidence suggests this practice has been largely unbroken, each year, since 2500 B.C., according to *Chan Kei Thong in Faith of Our Fathers*. Other evidence shows that Nestorian missionaries may have converted one or two Chinese emperors to a form of Christianity in the ninth century.

Until recently, the God I knew mostly worked in Europe or the United States. The God of my childhood was very active in the first century, but seemed to take a vacation and got active again with the advent of Protestants and the English Bible in the 16th century. The God I knew in seminary left non-western countries pretty much alone until they were either colonized by the West or had Western missionaries visit them.

When I first moved to Washington, D.C. after college, I stayed with an older couple who had lived on a cul-de-sac for 25 years, playing cards with their neighbors every Friday for all of those years. These neighbors raised their children together, attended church together, and sometimes took each other to work. After 25 years, they both retired on the same day and told their neighbors that for the whole 25 years they had been telling them a lie about working for the State Department, even to the point of having them "drop them off" at the State Department headquarters in Washington DC. They were actually CIA employees at the CIA McLean headquarters. The shock was so great that it took the neighbors several years to trust them again. Some never recovered.

For me, learning that God had been very active for centuries in cultures that I didn't know about made me feel like one of these neighbors. I felt betrayed at first. I thought I was the favorite child in a small family and suddenly I realized my Father has families all over the place that He loves as much as mine. After a time of denial and jealousy, I then started getting more curious. What stories did these my distant siblings know about my Father that I didn't know? As I began to ask them to tell me these stories, it became apparent to me that my Father was a much bigger and more loving Person than I had ever imagined.

For Western Christians, these countries provide new pieces to the puzzle that Christians in the West have never seen before. It is like having two blind men spending years exploring the elephant—then suddenly realize there are four more blind men, each of whom have been standing in a different place for all those years seeking the same thing. The new explorers come with worlds of new information about our God who is so much larger than what any one culture can experience fully.

We live in a time like no other when the "blind men" in various cultures can talk together. Just as the Roman roads in the first century allowed the gospel to spread quickly, even greater openings have occurred in the last 50 years:

(1) the breakdown of the colonial system so that there is more respect and better "hearing" of what Christians in developing countries bring to the dialogue

(2) increasingly less-expensive air travel causing more people to travel cross-culturally than ever before

(3) a global economy so that relationships and connections across culture have become part of most people's daily life experience

(4) the Internet that allows instantaneous and easily accessible global information and communication

(5) postmodernism—the eroding of overconfidence in literary, rational-based cultures so that cultures who use oral learning or mystical routes to seek God are increasingly respected

Yet perhaps most amazing is:

(1) the advent of the global city as the experience of the majority of the world.

The global city means that the conversation between blind men does not have to involve long trips, global summits, or dramatic, extensive effort. It means the pooling of our partial knowledge of God in conversations that occur in everyday life, in our own backyards, in ways that are often mundane yet profound. In our daily lives of working at the office, going to the grocery store, and walking in our neighborhoods, we often have more access to other cultures in a few hours than the great explorers of previous centuries experienced in a lifetime. This means we can "see" and worship God with an ever-expanding perspective by being good listeners in the everyday life of the global city where we live.

The tendency remains for all of us to insist that how *we* see God is the most accurate of all. However, with the advent of unprecedented global connections in the recent decades, there has never been a better opportunity for us "blind men" to compare our notes. As we do, we are finding ourselves more confused than ever as we realize that what we thought was a whole picture of God from *our* cultural perspective is merely a small part of what we might see. We are more in awe of the Person we are seeking and more dependent on people of other cultures to help us in our theological quest. Theology is increasingly more about asking questions of the very people that we used to ignore or even argue against.

Yet spiritual formation doesn't stop at merely trying to understand the bigness of God. This spiritual formation must move us to the worship of this God, who we previously thought was smaller and more controllable.

Global Cities Propel Us to New Heights of Worship

As I travel in Europe, I am amazed at the great effort medieval Christians put into building cathedrals. Thousands of lives were spent over many years to build spaces that remind us of the greatness and power of God. In most of these cathedrals, your eye is immediately drawn upward to grandeur and beauty that instantly shocks you into the realization that you have estimated God too lowly and yourself too highly. The space itself creates awe, mystery, and a reverence that allows you to be aware of God's presence and power.

When approached with the right perspective, the city can become our new cathedrals. The complexity, confusion, and frustration of the space constantly remind us of our inadequacy. Yet the beauty of the relationships and the transformed lives that we see in these places where beauty and transformation seem so unlikely create an awe, mystery, and reverence that lets us know that God is present and powerful.

The global city provides unprecedented access to worldwide history and current events, at a scale never before possible, that can lead us to worship in ways never before possible. Let us be a people always in search of the grand and magnificent elephant and never satisfied by finding a tree, wall, rope, or snake.

■ ■ ■ Personal Reflection

What are some cross-cultural experiences you've had—either by traveling to another culture or experiencing another culture in your own city? Pick one that was either the most extensive or intense.

What was uncomfortable about this experience?

What was exciting about this experience?

What insight did you gain from this experience?

What did it make you more critical of and more appreciative of in your home culture?

If you experienced this with others, how did you see them respond, and what did they learn?

Business or vacation travel experiences are often not as structured as short-term mission trips with time for reflection about what you are learning about God during the experience. However, they can be just as powerful if you take time for intentional reflection. Can you describe how such an experience caused you to:

Be disrupted in ways that formed a bigger view of God?

Become aware of God's goodness and power in ways that spurred worship?

Learn new insights about God from the people and culture you visited?

■ ■ ■ Bible Reflection

In Matthew 28 and Acts 1, God specifically commands us to take the gospel to the whole world. Why is the global sharing of the gospel such an important part of what God calls us to do?

Why is it an essential part of what Jesus commands a disciple to do?

Revelation 7 describes an experience in which people from every nation and every tribe participate in worshipping God. In preceding chapters of Revelation, the throne room of God is described as being inhabited by a variety of creatures of different types. Why is variety and diversity such an important theme in the throne room of God?

Would you say the biblical commands of Matthew 28 and Acts 1 to go to the whole world are more about:

Strategy—how God plans to advance the gospel;

Discipleship—how we are formed through mission; or

Worship—how we understand God's power and goodness?

Explain why.

What difference does your answer make in your life?

Chapter Three: CHANGING WORLD, CHANGING CHURCH

Spiritual Formation Principle #3: God forms us through His church, but it may be a different form of church than what we have been used to in the past.

Theme: The church is not simply a Sunday morning program in a specific building, but primarily a community of people dependent on God, immersed throughout the world, with the deep courage to face both joy and pain.

Bible Reading:
Genesis 3:14–24
Mark 8:34–38
Romans 8:18–29

Urban Ministry as Life-Art

In high school, I worked as a part-time guard in the Houston Museum of Fine Arts. My mother, a postmodern abstract-expressionist artist, often taught in the museum. My semi-retired grandfather supervised the museum guards. I needed some extra cash during the school year and being a guard seemed much better than my summer construction job in Houston's heat.

My mom and grandfather often asked me in which room I wanted to be stationed. I always said that I wanted to be in the room that displayed Impressionist art. There I stood for hours in galleries rarely visited on week nights, watching for suspicious characters who might yield to the temptation to poke an oily finger onto a canvas. But in the quiet and loneliness, I would stare for hours at three Vincent Van Gogh paintings. They had vibrant colors, wildly swirling pallet knife strokes, reckless textures, and shadows of light and dark that changed dramatically as you walked nearer or farther from each of the paintings. Somehow, knowing the story of this artist's life and death made the paintings more courageous to me.

Van Gogh spent much of 1889 in the asylum at Saint-Rémy-de-Mausole, where he completed 142 works. Right before his suicide in 1890, Van Gogh visited his brother, who was experiencing a painful situation with his work that threatened the financial future of Van Gogh and his brother's young family. *Van Gogh in Provence and Auvers* by Bogomila Welsh-Ovcharov records that as Van Gogh painted the last paintings before his suicide, he wrote his brother, Theo,

> "I began to paint again, even though I could barely hold the brush, but knowing exactly what I wanted to paint, I began three more large canvases . . . of large wheat fields under cloudy skies, and it did not take a great deal to express sadness and loneliness. . . . I believe these paintings say what words cannot."
>
> —VINCENT VAN GOGH,
> quoted in *Van Gogh in Provence and Auvers*

The great poets, songwriters, novelists, and other artists don't try to fix or understand this pain. At first, they find solace in just expressing it and sharing their expression with others. Yet for some, their expression becomes a life-journey of deepening despair. Why is the pain there? Why is it so profound? Why does the pain grow deeper and deeper the more I stare into it? For some, what started as a day's hike into an unexplored cavern becomes a lifetime labyrinth of increasing confusion and deepening pain. The great artists are some of the most courageous humans on earth. We value their expressions as windows into places of mystery we don't dare to go ourselves.

The great artists don't always paint or write about pain. Some are courageous to explore their dreams. I imagine that they wonder, *What does this better place that I can imagine actually look like? What would happen if I extrapolate the actual small joys I find in my life to a place in my imagination where joy is overwhelming? Then why does it make me feel the pain of my existence deeper when I spend time seeking the limits of the joy in my imagination?*

Every human heart feels the constant pain of the awareness of a better state than what we are experiencing. Revolutions are started not when things are very bad, but when people have the expectation and hope that things could be better. It is not severe circumstances that create revolutions, but the distance between expectations and reality. We have a hard time living in the space between an existence that is painful and dreams that stir the desires of our hearts.

It is not surprising that the starting place of every major philosophy and religion starts with the question, "Why can I imagine such a better state than what I live in?" Recognizing that the statements below grossly oversimplify centuries of deep thought, some examples might include:

- The Buddhist, who would say, "The state I feel is not reality. The material world is an illusion. When I remove myself from the passions of the material world I will find that what I am imagining as a better state in my meditations and trances is the actual reality."

- The Hindu, who would say, "What I experience now is merely part of the journey toward the better state that I can imagine. If I submit to my place along my path in this life today, I will progress to a better place on that path in my next life tomorrow."

- The New Age-er, who would say, "What we imagine as a better state is the force of collective human imagination. It will become real if we all bend our wills and actions toward it."

- The Christian would say, "We were created to live in a Garden (or ideal existence) in God's presence. We chose not to trust God (Genesis 3). We were evicted from the Garden. That was meaningless if we are in rebellion against God. The natural consequences of our choice were death and futility—actually *gifts* in disguise to give us reason to choose to return to God and our true place in the universe. Now all humans live in a fallen world and face the painful circumstances of our choice. We are all born with the powerful, passionate, internal desires of being Garden-creatures. But we face the pain of living in a ghetto. It is not our natural habitat. We, and all of creation with us, groan inwardly, waiting for us all to be returned to the state for which we were created." (See Romans 8:22–23.) How each of us deals with this churning pain of the heart defines much of our life.

- For some, a life of inane busyness keeps them distracted.
- For some, alcoholism, drug abuse, sexual or other addictions blur their senses from completely feeling the pain of being fallen.
- For some, a life in the fantasy world of daydreams, video games, romance novels, celebrity lifestyles, and sports heroes provides wonderful hours of solace.
- For some, a key relationship—spouse, child, parent, friend—is the antidote to the pain. Yet that key person always disappoints, often fleeing from the pain-medication role they could never fulfill.

For some, gaining and using money to create little counterfeit gardens creates a constant carrot on a stick of hope that keeps their eyes focused ahead, away from the pain. The world economy is driven by this hope. There is some golden purchase, some exciting experience, some inkling of fame or comfort just around the next corner that chasers hope will stop the ache. The celebrities, who we obsess over, dress and live in ways that give us concrete pictures of that for which we hope. We work hard to gain a suburban life with high fences, miniature mansions, and pristine malls, in order to taste this hope in our own lives. The carrot is always just inches in front of us, but we can never seem to touch it.

Face Painting

The suburban experience not only doesn't deliver; it rarely promises what we want. Perhaps that is why some people without the talent of a songwriter or canvas artist instead venture into the city. This becomes their courageous, artistic journey of life-art; the medium of their art is life. They paint not with oils, but with experiences. Their face becomes their canvas. There is profound beauty in the depth of their gaze, the quietness of their manner; the ability to stare unblinking into pain and their lack of shame to shed a tear.

There is something about living where pain is stared at without blinking that builds a unique strength in a person's life. I know many long-term urban ministers who are also artists, poets, songwriters, and writers. It doesn't surprise me how urban-based art such as rap is so attractive to people who don't live in urban centers. Urban-based sitcoms and adventure shows dominate television and movies. People in suburban malls flock to clothing retailers to get an urban look. Others want to *look like* those who are not afraid of pain but they don't want to go through the actual journey to *be* one of those people.

Urban ministry is one of the many ways people choose to move toward pain in order to find God in a deeper way. Yet the same journey can happen in other ways that we don't choose; in crises of relationships, health, work, and family. The key is what we do with the pain. Are we scared of it? Do we want to act as though it doesn't exist? Do we want to keep ourselves distracted from feeling the pain? Or do we decide that pain is the journey of spiritual formation that God has appointed, and move squarely into it? Do we choose to find our joy in the character of God, even though every circumstance tells us to despair?

This artistic journey to explore pain is best pursued in a community of courageous colleagues. The richest community should grow among the lives of those who don't flinch in the face of pain. Yet, the saddest reality I know is that the very community that is best prepared to create this kind of life-art on the canvasses of the faces of their people is often the most effective at creating escapes; the church. The church was meant to be that community of courageous colleagues but, for many of us, we've experienced churches that were very far from what they were intended to be.

Emotional Impairment

In 1991, I planted a church in a neighborhood in the shadow of the skyscrapers of downtown Dallas. It was one of the few neighborhoods in this Bible-belt city where people sought an enclave where they could feel free from Bible-talk. Here they could find a safe place with like-minded people who didn't go to church on Sunday morning, and who were proud of that. Yet, like all people, they craved community and the attempt to build an "anti-Dallas, anti-church" society did not satisfy all of them. So they slowly began showing up at our community events: chili cook-offs; homemade ice-cream-offs; volleyball games; band gigs; neighborhood cleanups; afterschool tutoring; and assorted urban ministries. From there, even more slowly, they began to show up in our Sunday morning services that were held in a rented art gallery.

One morning, I used an illustration of a *Far Side* cartoon in my sermon. In the cartoon, there were wolves on the outside ring of a campfire. Close to the fire were a few cowboys and one of their former wolf comrades. The wolves on the outskirts were saying that their comrade had become "domesticated." After the sermon, five or six people came up to me and said, "That cartoon you talked about is exactly how I see most churches. People go there, put on fake smiles, and remove themselves from reality. It is like 'happy land' and those of us who can't fake it—or don't want to—are not welcome. If becoming a Christian means getting an emotional lobotomy, then I want no part of it."

I realized that afternoon that, while I could pick a good illustration, my life of growing up in a Christian subculture and the choices I made in that subculture had made me "domesticated." I was emotionally impaired. If I couldn't face pain myself or if I was scared of true celebration, then I was never going to pastor a church that could draw in nonChristians who thought Christians were emotionally lobotomized. The next day, I called up a friend who was a counselor and said "Sign me up; I need help." That started an amazing multi-year journey of destroying layers of force fields that I had ingeniously built over many years to stand against feeling intense pain and profound joy. I did not want those capacities.

I've always wondered why Christ followers did not invent grunge rock . . . and bubble gum-pop rock. It seems odd that Christian music is often five years behind the cutting edge of the rest of the music scene rather than leading it. Of all people, we who have the hope of a God who sustains us in the deepest of pain and the greatest of joys should be the ones who have the freedom to produce art at both extremes.

Several years ago, my brother upgraded his stereo receiver before he had money to upgrade his speakers. The receiver had the capacity to project higher highs and lower lows than what the speakers could handle. So he kept the volume low to avoid the inevitable . . . until one day when my curious four-year-old nephew turned up the volume knob. By the time my brother arrived in the den, the speakers were smoking and destroyed.

Perhaps this is a metaphor for how many Christians feel. Like any human, we feel fragile. We are afraid of pain, but also equally afraid of too much happiness. We do what we can to avoid pain and sabotage ourselves when it looks like things are getting too good. Then we collect ourselves into a community of like-minded people committed to the same. Sometimes that is called a church. Avoiding pain and disappointment becomes a tragic misappropriation of the church, which is God's hope for the world. It is not what the church was intended to be.

Urbanologist Ray Bakke says the widespread change in our world "challenges very fundamental practices of the church; even more, theological ways of thinking about the nature and mission of the church, and this is true on all 6 continents now." The city gathers people into communities, such as skyscrapers and airports, which remain unreachable to traditional forms of institutional church. The city creates a need for new strategies for the church. But there is more than just layering on new strategies to the myriad of church programs we already have. Before we can have new strategies, we need to reclaim the identity of what *church* actually is.

What is *church*?

Close your eyes. Say *church*. What picture comes to your mind? When five people do this, it is likely that they have five very different pictures in their heads. *Church* has become one of those words that is used to mean so many different things that, as rich as its original meaning, today it is an almost shallow, meaningless word.

For example, I am not a traditional learner. I learn more by questioning, observation, immersion, relationships, and dialogue rather than reading. I am much better at creating adult learning experiences—events that use a combination of reading, hands-on experience, peer discussions, and personal reflection—not simply gathering content, but learning a new perspective. During a recent event, we drove senior pastors and executive pastors of large churches to one of the largest church campuses in the world. The building has 800,000 square feet, an auditorium for 7,500 on Sunday morning, a restaurant, school for 1,400 students, workout facilities, gyms, and a football stadium. The campus is on 140 acres and to-date has costs about $140 million to develop. A mirror campus 14 miles to the north is currently being developed that, when finished, will cost about as much as the original. The plan at that point is to have two worship services, but video the preacher on one campus and broadcast him to the other campus on a large screen.

The executive pastor of the church, who hosted our group, used a PowerPoint presentation to explain the 57 key functions in his job description. The church has more than 500 staff members and almost all of the 57 functions involved the coordination of the people and programs of the church. An intern then gave us a tour of the facility. He showed us the $1 million row of stained glass in the foyer and a choir room for 600 that he described as "larger than most churches in America." The church has more than 500 Bible Study classes, but is organized in a way that no church-sponsored small groups or classes meet outside of the central campus, even during the week. We all were awed by the immensity and excellence of the building, programs, and professionalism of the staff.

The next morning, I led a discussion on what the word *church* means in the Bible, a summary of which I've included in the next section. That afternoon we visited a smaller church called Irving Bible Church (IBC) that has an auditorium with 2,500 seats, a school, and a cafe. This time the executive pastor Steve Roese led a free-form informal discussion responding to our questions. When asked about their building, he replied,

> "We are not a church that makes a big deal about our building. As a matter of fact, we realize it was necessary to build this building to accommodate our growth, but after we moved in, I think our whole staff was depressed for 18 months. We designed this building more as a public park with one of the best indoor playgrounds in north Texas. Over 60 percent of people who rent it do so for children's birthday parties and do not attend our church. People come in here and tell us their real estate agent said having this park near their house would increase their property values. We also have a café with free Wi-fi Internet for local business people to come over when they need to get away from their offices and it is well used by people who also don't attend our church. The park opens at 7 A.M. and closes at 10 P.M. every day and the people around here get quite upset if *their* park is not open on time. The offices, audio equipment, and day school are in secure zones away from the public zones.
>
> "As a matter of fact, we are thinking about renaming our building to something that has the word 'park' in it, then call ourselves 'The Church that meets at _____ Park'. It is very important to us that people don't think of our church as this building. The church is the people who meet here and then live their lives throughout the city."

The stark contrast between the two churches gave us all a fresh understanding of how various churches define their identity. The first church demonstrated a community of believers that built their community around a building. This example has many strengths. Yet this church has to be on constant guard that the building does not become its primary identity. In contrast, IBC demonstrated a community of believers that was so concerned that the building serves the people that they worked very hard to use the word *church* only to mean the *community*, not the building. The building was both named and designed to support the church, not to be the church

What IBC recognized is that most people associate the word *church* with a:

(1) legal organization to which you give tax-deductible donations;

(2) Sunday morning program of teaching, worship, and education; and

(3) a specific building.

Yet in the New Testament, the word *church* is refers to one of the following:

(1) The "universal" church: every follower of Christ, in every location and every period of history from Pentecost (Acts 2) to the present

(2) a "local" church that is in one location and time period; the subset of #1 above. In the New Testament epistles and Revelation 2 and 3, local churches are called "The church in ___ city". During that era, cities were smaller and the church was very small (possibly under 100 people in some of these cities) so there were not multiple churches in one city. Thus the church in Ephesus meant the whole community of Christ followers who lived in Ephesus.

(3) An "apostolic band": Some people argue that groups of apostles such as Paul, Peter, and others who traveled between local churches is another way the word *church* is used in the New Testament. Since that time, this aspect of the church is expressed in orders and parachurch ministries that concentrate on specific works of the church, such as church planting, disaster relief, evangelism, and so on.

Originally, a community of believers met in houses, caves, and catacombs—sometimes moving around to avoid persecution. In that early era, it was easy for the word *church* to refer to a community of believers since there were few buildings, programs, or institutions. However, over the centuries, *church* began to refer more to the institutions that were created to organize the community rather than the actual community of believers itself. As these institutions took different directions, the word became modified by words like *Catholic*, *Orthodox*, and *Protestant*, and later by further subsets such as *Methodist*, *Baptist*, *Coptic*, and so on. As buildings were built to house these communities, *church* began to refer more to the building than the people inside. And finally, as the activities of the institution became more focused on Sunday morning, *church* began also to refer to the set of programs the institution produced on Sunday morning. So today it is not unusual for someone to use the word *church* to mean:

(1) An institution: "I am a member of the Presbyterian church";

(2) A building: "I attend the church located at Westford and Pine."

(3) A set of programs: "I am going to church on Sunday morning."

There is nothing wrong with institutions, buildings, and programs. All three are essential to serve a larger community of believers. What creates a problem is when these structures that were designed to support the community become the goal rather than the means. Today, many people cannot imagine what a church would actually look like if it did not have institutions, buildings, and programs. As a result, too often church leaders see their purpose in church is to use people to support the structures rather than use the structures to support the people. Some indication that this has happened might include:

(1) When a large percentage (above 80 percent) of the money, time, and energy of the church community is used to pay for the building and staff needed to produce Sunday morning programs.

(2) When words like *worship*, *community*, and *prayer* refer more often to programs produced by the church staff rather than something that all believers

are engaged in throughout the week—in their families, neighborhoods, work-places—in ways that have little to do with organized programs.

(3) When church leaders spend the majority of their time making decisions about buildings, programs, and budgets

(4) When the community of believers is so busy doing buildings, institutions, and programs that they don't care greatly for each other, don't reach out significantly to their neighbors, and they experience burnout of activity rather than the fire of the Holy Spirit.

And especially—

(5) When it becomes hard to imagine new forms of church that are not centered on institutions, buildings, and programs.

It is my experience that most pastors and church leaders worry about this a great deal and many are frustrated by the seemingly unstoppable momentum of institutions, buildings, and programs. Some feel that our current culture has so misunderstood the word and work of the *church* that they are fighting an almost impossible gravitational pull against returning the church to its true meaning and purpose. Others realize they have a responsibility to lead the community of people, but their work is actually measured by how well they organize the institution, buildings, and programs. Since institutions, buildings, and programs are necessary means to build health in a larger community of people, it is confusing at times which is serving which.

How would you measure church leadership? What if we measured by how well they help their people engage in a courageous art-journey? Can you quantifiably measure life-art? Can you objectify whether one face displays more tears and broader smiles than another; unflinchingly facing the deepest of pain and the heights of joy? These are the questions with which many pastors and church leaders struggle. In absence of solutions, they feel trapped on a treadmill of having to focus on institutions, buildings, and programs. And many of the people they lead feel the same. Over time, the trap becomes the reality and everyone forgets from what they were fighting so hard to get free.

In attempts to separate these wrong definitions of *church* from its true meaning, some people refer to the *institutional* church as opposed to the church. The first refers to the structures, the second is the people. Ray Stedman described the church as being expressed in two ways:

(1) The church "gathered"—often meeting on Sunday morning, or throughout the week in small groups, often being gathered in buildings or by programs that leaders in the church community have organized

(2) The church "scattered"—individual believers or small groups of believers in families, neighborhoods, and workplaces *being* the church in ways that are not organized or programmed by leaders of the church community

During the last two decades, many leaders have attempted to correct misunderstandings about the word *church* by attaching a label in front of the word. In 2000, I was up against a marketing deadline to name a conference we were producing at Leadership Network. Our conference was attached to another conference at Windsor Village United Methodist Church in Houston called "The E-Church." The point of the conference was to use the example of Windsor Village to help church leaders learn how to go beyond Sunday morning church programming to reach out to their community.

Starting in the late 1990s, the term *missional* church came to be used to describe the church that reacts to seeing God's character by being on mission with Him. The missional church theological movement discussed missions as the core purpose of people made in the image of God; individuals such as Abraham called by God, and the people of Israel in the Old Testament and the church in the New Testament. I didn't want to call the conference a *missional church* conference because that would confuse the practice of the missional church with its founding theology and principles. This was a conference focused on *practices* that flowed from the *principles.*

I had been working with Sue Mallory right at that time on a book titled *The Equipping Church* and I was trying to coordinate the title of this conference to the "e" theme so I had "e" on my brain. About 10 P.M. I came up with the phrase "Externally-focused Church" so I wrote an e-mail to our marketing director to say to go with that title. I didn't really like it, but there was the deadline. Then as the conference neared and people started telling us how much they liked the title, I became afraid that I had created a monster. When I introduced the conference, I expressed my sorrow that we would have to use a descriptor such as *externally focused* before the word *church*. If we really understood the word *church*, we wouldn't have to modify it with externally focused any more than we have to say a "female woman" or "wet water." God never intended for the church to take on the meaning or practice of a country club that does programs to serve only its members. *Church* should mean a community of believers actively serving others in the world.

Since that time, of course, we did several more versions of that conference using the same name. My friend Eric Swanson, who was on staff at Leadership Network, has coauthored a fantastic book using that title. The book focuses on local community service and I pass it out like candy. Eric recently graduated from Bakke Graduate University where I became employed. He has taken the original ideas far beyond what any of us imagined. We use the term "externally-focused church" in our classes as it applies to the six areas of possible programming focus for the church outside of its Sunday morning programs that we identified in that original conference. They are:

(1) Service in the local community and city
(2) Global missions
(3) The family in society-at-large
(4) The workplace
(5) Government and the public square
(6) Popular culture—entertainment, sports, and so on.

But I still wince a bit when I hear the phrase. Yet, I am not the only one who has modified *church* with what should be redundant qualifiers. Others agree we've lost much of the meaning of the word *church* and so they have modified it with qualifiers such as:

(1) a purpose-driven church—one that is focused on the five purposes of Matt. 28

(2) an equipping church—one that is focused on equipping people to serve as described in Ephesians 4

(3) a missional church—one that understands God is a missional God and the church should reflect that aspect of His character, or

(4) an organic church—one that is built more around people and internal values than programs and structures.

The point is that, while most of us know that the formal definition of *church* means a community of Christ followers, we actually use the word to mean many other things. When we say we want to "change the church," we really mean we want to change the institutions, buildings, and programs that are the current expressions of the church. The church is the hope of the world. It is God's gift to the world as all nature groans waiting for the sons of God to be revealed (Romans 8:22). We cannot assume that the old institutions, buildings, and programs attached to the urban church are the hope of the urban world.

The Church May Be Further Along Than We Realize

If we define *church* as what happens on Sunday morning in buildings with steeples, then its future in the city looks gloomy. Even if we add a modifier to the word, such as *externally focused* or *purpose-driven*, the phrase still ends with a word that conveys institutions, buildings, and programs rather than a "community of Christ followers."

Ray Bakke essentially says that widespread changes in our world should cause new changes in our church. He identifies the reality that there are high-rise office and residential buildings, airports, and other structures that need whole new types of church plants to reach them. Ray identifies the migratory, psychological, and financial challenges of the city that traditional forms of the institutional church cannot meet well.

In reality, the community of Christ followers is already participating deeply in these changes, in their workplaces, neighborhoods, and lifestyles. When we define the church as the community of Christ followers, we suddenly realize that the church is deeply planted in every skyscraper, every airport, employee pool, every workplace, school, and every neighborhood in the city—even those totally inaccessible by the institutional church.

If you are shooting an arrow and consistently miss the target to the left, the easiest way to fix that problem would be to untack the paper target, move it left, and place it over the area where you *are* hitting. What needs to be changed are the institutions, programs, and buildings that should support these communities of Christ followers as they live out the gospel in the middle of our fast-changing world.

I have heard several speakers in recent years say, "There are places in the world that are more church-like than the church." It is a catchy phrase but I think I am more comfortable with saying, "The church remains the hope of the world, so we need to change our definition and practice of church to prove it." God is causing the transformation that He intended all along. We become successful when we move our definitions and focus onto what God is already doing.

No amount of church bureaucracy, misspent millions on ridiculously gaudy buildings, or wasted hours in church committee meetings will deter Christ from accomplishing His purposes through the church. These things will, however, keep some of us from the art-journey God intended. That is the tragedy for some of us, but it doesn't stop God. Even if these supporting institutions, buildings, and programs don't change, the community of Christ followers will remain the hope of the world.

Steps to Becoming an Art Community

The first step in changing the definition of *church* is to change the definition of what a Christ-follower is. I think the metaphor of *artist* is a much better illustration of a Christ follower than the metaphor of a "superhero," a "Mr. Fix It," or even a "benevolent rich aunt." We have a great deal of power in the institutions, buildings, and programs that we call the church. If you are reading this book, you are probably educated, have some money to invest, and can recruit other educated people with some money too. We can use that power to fix a lot of problems and to make life better for others and to make ourselves feel good in the process. There is nothing wrong with that, and all of those things should happen. But they shouldn't be our only goal, or even our primary goal. Using our power, education, and money to fix things cheapens what it means for us to be made in God's image; it cheapens the image of God in those whom we serve. Thankfully, God is committed to not allowing us to cheapen ourselves and others.

It helps to know that in the big picture, we are called to transform our world, but *we* will not be successful in doing this. The Book of Revelation shows a world in rebellion and chaos. In chapter 19, Christ returns on a white horse with a sword in His mouth. *That* is when the world is fully transformed.

Many have communicated that since we can't fix the world, we should avoid the world—which reflects a "superhero" identity, but these "superheroes" live in exile. Others say, if we could only work harder, pray more, or organize better, we could fix the world. This reflects a "superhero" self-identity; constantly banging our heads on a steel wall, hoping against hope that someday the steel will prove softer than our heads.

Yet an artist doesn't actually think that he or she can fix the world. An artist's job is to try as much as possible to fix it, but never expect to be totally successful. So artists express the joy and the pain of what it feels like to be in that journey. And others are drawn to their artistry because they realize the artists are courageous enough to stay in the journey, even though they cannot control the outcome.

Many people get into urban ministry with the hope of finding a new personal significance in the many heroic things they accomplish for the good of others. Some have a false image that people are waiting in the ghetto for well-meaning people to arrive and to help them out of their plight by teaching them new ways to think and live. We all feel insignificant every day. We all feel the pain of relationships that fall short of our hopes every day. It seems logical that if we go to a place where people need what we have to offer that we will feel significant in helping them and connected with them as they express gratitude for our help.

There are times when we *do* receive gratitude, especially in urban ministry activities that involve younger children. There are times this happens when your host in the ghetto is an alive and vibrant city church. Even urban ministry conducted in short bursts—cleanup days, building homes, sports camps, strategy sessions, or joint worship services—can create a temporary joy of expectancy and accomplishment. Once you venture out beyond these ministries into a long-term commitment to the city and to relationships with those who live there, or even relocate there yourself, you may wonder what happened to those smiling faces and good feelings. You will quickly find there are systems of evil in the ghetto and in yourself that will overwhelm any hope of bolstering personal significance.

Saying that an artist is a metaphor for good urban ministry might seem ridiculous at first. Urban ministry should be about persevering against all hardships to obtain results that transform people and places. It should be about stubbornly clinging to a goal in spite of all obstacles. A metaphor of a football game in a mud field in the middle of a sweltering Texas August sounds much more appropriate than what might appear to some as the seemingly frivolous, self-absorbed, air-conditioned work of an artist.

Perhaps most people have never seen a truly great artist. This is not the weekend artist who paints by the numbers or uses a glue gun to apply appliqués to a jeans jacket. It is the serious artist who journeys headlong into the deepest experiences to find the deepest emotions within herself to express. More importantly the metaphor reminds us that the heart of urban ministry is *not* about scoring points, making the goal line, and forcing what we know is best on the opposing team—often the very people to whom we are ministering. Urban ministry is about living well in the futility of the fallen world, and finding great joy without diminishing the deepest pain. Amazingly, it is the life lived this way that is most effective in urban ministry. People, neighborhoods, cities, economies, and nations are transformed by the relationships formed by people who are great life-artists. Not surprisingly, this same life-art is effective in just about ever other place as well.

Great art is not produced by a formula. First, it comes from living deeply. Then the brush strokes, colors, and textures come in the right places at the right time. Urban ministry also flows from living deeply. There are no formulas for when to angrily confront an armed drug dealer on a street corner, or when to lie down, crying, on top of a 13-year-old about to receive a life-stealing cut in a gang fight. For those who live deeply, the right action comes at the right time, and it is such a natural outflow of the life that has deep impact on others. You can't specifically plan ahead for the most powerful moments of urban ministry, but you can prepare your life by not flinching from pain each day. When pain comes in the context of a defining moment in urban ministry, you don't blink, and everyone who watches knows that nobody can fake that.

The second step is to join or form a community willing to walk toward pain, not hide from it. The way you find such a group is to start the journey. The others will find you—colleagues at work; fellow urban-ministry volunteers; people living in the city who have the power to move out but choose to stay. If the institution, building, and programs that you call "my church" are not willing to support you in this journey, pray for another community of believers who *are* willing. There are still many reasons to stay connected to the institution you call "my church." But after reading this chapter, it is my hope that you are less apologetic about spending more time with a community of Christ followers who choose to organize themselves less institutionally. Both the institutional and noninstitutional expressions of your church can add valuable life-support in your art journey.

The third step is to look for natural connection points for urban ministry. These may start with urban ministry programs, but programs are at best merely incubators for relationships. The relationships that form are what create the real connection points. We will discuss this in later chapters, but look for where God has preceded your work—not by plans, strategies, success stories, easy routes, or good ideas, but by relationships that seem to grow in ways that defy logic.

Ultimately, good art is not about the resulting forms on the canvas, but about the relationship between the artist and the subjects of painting. If the relationship is strained, the canvas will project flatness. If the object is profoundly interesting to the artist, the canvas will be profoundly interesting to the viewer. The artist does not set out to change the subject, but to experience it. Yet, when that object is painted with great passion, no one who ever looks on the original object will ever see it in the same way again. The object is profoundly changed in the eyes of others. And if the painting is a portrait, often the one painted is changed forever as he or she looks at how the artist has reflected back to them not a mirror image, but an image that shows the relationship. And relationships, experienced and expressed, are what change all of us, whether will live in the ghetto or the gated community.

■ ■ ■ Personal Reflection

(1) It is a natural muscle reflex to dodge an action that will cause pain. It is also a natural lifestyle response for most of us to avoid painful situations whenever possible.

- Why is relearning this response in your life so important in urban ministry?

- Why is it so important in spiritual formation?

(2) One way to avoid a trial is to frantically scramble to overcome it. While the trial may remain, our frantic efforts can numb us from feeling it. Yet God often brings trials into our lives to teach us greater dependence and trust.

   • When do you find you have the courage of an artist—moving deeper into a painful circumstance without demanding that it be fixed?

(3) When have you experienced a time that you went against this tendency in training for sports, in pursuing a painful relationship, or practicing an uncomfortable discipline?

   • When has this purposeful movement toward pain caused you to grow?

   • When has it caused you scars that have not healed?

• What was different in the circumstances or your response in these situations?

• What joy have you found in the midst of pursuing that which can be painful?

■ ■ ■ Bible Reflection

(1) Read Genesis 3:14–24. Is the curse more about changing the nature of who Adam and Eve were, or more about changing the circumstances in which they lived? Express how they might have felt to be Garden-creatures suddenly evicted from the habitat for which they were created?

(2) Read Mark 8:34–38. Why do you think discipleship starts with dying to self? How do we do that when so many messages in our culture are about finding fulfillment of self? What are some actions we can take to start self-denial in deed, not just in word?

(3) Read Romans 8:18–29. It appears as if groaning is a reality of our whole world this side of heaven. Why do we work so hard at times to hide or deny the reality of groaning?

Chapter Four: GOD IS ALREADY PRESENT

Spiritual Formation Principle #4: We are spiritually formed not as much by what we do and say, but by how well we listen and follow where God has preceded us.

Theme: Urban ministry is less about meeting needs than it is about nurturing the strengths already present in the neighborhood.

Bible Reading:
Romans 1:18–25
Hebrews 11:1–13
Ephesians 2:8–10
James 1:19–25

Practice, Formation, and Theology

In this chapter, we want to understand the *principles* of good urban ministry *practice*. We also want to see how those ministry practices reflect spiritual formation that emerges from deep theological reflection.

Good urban ministry practice requires learning the uniqueness of the city and the communities where we serve. Each city has a distinct history and culture. As a result, we should seek to understand and to respect the people and capacities that are *already in the neighborhoods*. An important urban ministry practice is, therefore, to research the neighborhood before attempting to do urban ministry within it. The fact is, the solutions for the problems of individual city neighborhoods flow up from the grassroots leaders who are there and who are tailor-made for each of their locations.

This urban ministry practice corresponds to spiritual formation practices. God will form us spiritually through blessings, trials, relationships, leaders, and other things He brings into our lives, even if we are not intentional. However, spiritual formation is the practice of moving *intentionally* toward disciplines, activities, people, circumstances, and attitudes that cause us to be increasingly dependent and trusting of God. The hope is that our intentionality will increase our openness to God's work in our lives and move us to deeper dependence and trust of God.

Yet we also want to grow in our *theology*. The word means "the study of God." In the last few centuries, this has taken on new meanings as scientific methods were used in an attempt to study God. Unfortunately, *theology* is a confusing and inadequate word to capture this journey. Much theology has been written by people who don't think that a person must actually believe that God exists in order to be a good theologian.

However, many of us don't see the work of theology as an objective, detached study of God in the same way that, for example, entomology is the study of insects or ornithology is the study of birds. Most of us want to study God because we first *believe* in God, and we want to experience God in a greater way by learning more about Him. I hope that someone will invent in my lifetime a new word that describes the study of God as an immersion learning experience for all the senses, heart, and will. Until that time, we have to redefine the word *theology* to mean for us *a fuller understanding of God*.

Family Feud Between the East and the West

Early in the fourth century, a church leader named Arius of Alexandria taught that Jesus was not equal with God the Father, but instead was created by the Father. In

A.D. 325, the Council of Nicea condemned this teaching as heresy and in A.D. 381, the Council of Constantinople condemned a related view that the Holy Spirit was created by the Son. What emerged was the original language of the Nicean creed: "I believe in the Holy Spirit, the Lord and giver of life, who proceeds from the Father. Together with the Father and the Son He is adored and glorified."

However, the church in the West felt continued pressure by a form of Arianism in Germanic tribes living in the northern regions of Christianity. So to further emphasize the importance of the special role of Jesus in the Trinity, at the Third Council of Toledo in 589, the Western church added a phrase to the Nicene creed so that it read the "Holy Spirit proceeds from the Father *and the Son*. This additional phrase in Latin is pronounced *filioque*.

The Eastern church never accepted the addition of the filioque clause. Two centuries later, the Eastern church, surrounded by the emerging Islam religion, was under pressure to emphasize the preeminent role of God the Father within the Trinity. In what is now called the Filioque Debate, the eastern patriarch of Constantinople objected to the addition of "and the Son" The addition of that clause has been a primary source of division between the Eastern Orthodox and the Western Catholic church ever since.

When I first learned of the Filioque Debate, I thought several centuries of arguments about the addition of the words "and the Son" seemed trivial. Yet, these few words—along with the addition of very different cultures between the East and the West over many centuries—have created a major difference in how the Eastern and Western church understand how to do mission.

For example, in the book, *Orthodox Alaska*, Russian Orthodox priest Michael Oleska, explains how he views the difference. When Russian Orthodox missionaries arrived in Alaska in 1784, they assumed God had purposely created the lands and the people they found there. Since *their* Nicean Creed said the Holy Spirit is sent by the Father, they also believed the Holy Spirit already present had influenced the culture, stories, and faith of the people that lived in Alaska for centuries. They believed that the Holy Spirit could be active in shaping culture and revealing God's character and preparing saving grace.

With this belief, and with a different Nicean Creed, Michael Oleska tells the story of how the Russian Orthodox missionaries started their missionary work by asking questions about the people's culture and legends *before* telling them about Jesus and the Russian church. Oleska said that they were not surprised to learn of a sacrifice story among many of the Alaskan native tribes. He writes,

> "The bowhead whale, for example, is a huge and powerful crea-ture, perfectly capable of escaping a small skin boat paddled by a dozen men. To catch a whale, the hunters need the cooperation of their prey. It must not swim away. It must not dive to the ocean depths. It must not attack. It must float on the surface and wait for the hunters to arrive, then allow them to maneuver their tiny boat directly in front of its head, and permit them to throw their hand-made harpoons directly into its face. . . . The Eskimo [belief] is that whales allow themselves to be killed, trusting that the People will treat them respectfully and allow them to be reborn."

The Russian Orthodox missionaries believed that God had prepared the Alaskan native people through the story of the sacrificial whale to understand and accept the story of Jesus, the sacrificial lamb of God. Alaskan natives (Inuit and Yupik) had never seen sheep or lambs so it would take as much time and faith to explain to them what a lamb was as it took for them to hear about the name and work of Jesus. So the missionaries explained that God had brought these whales to them not only to give them physical salvation for the winter, but also to prepare a way for them to learn about how God had prepared His Son to be their spiritual salvation for eternity. Thus, to Alaskan natives, Jesus was God's sacrificial whale offering eternal salvation.

There is much to celebrate and critique about both the Orthodox and Protestant mission work in Alaska. But the purpose here is to illustrate that wherever *we* go to minister, our omnipresent God has already been active in revealing His character. This principle has been confirmed by God's work in biblical times and in the world today; in the 4,000 year-old culture of China, as Thong Chan Kai writes in *Faith of Our Fathers*, and in many other cultures throughout the world.

Scripture confirms that it is not simply our initiative to minister, but God's work that preceeds us that allows for others' salvation and spiritual formation.

> *"No one can come to me unless the Father who sent me draws him, and I will raise him up at the last day. It is written in the Prophets: 'They will all be taught by God.' Everyone who listens to the Father and learns from him comes to me."*
>
> —JOHN 6:44–45

I grew up in a strong Bible tradition. We had missionaries in our church and home, who spent their lives living among remote tribes and translating the Bible into native languages for the purpose of evangelism. I learned a lot about the danger of syncretism when Christians adapted both Christian beliefs along with pagan beliefs. The dangers of syncretism are real. These Bible translators are great heroes of my past and present. They opened new doors of faith and discipleship that did not exist before they arrived. They were instruments of God to reveal His specific work of grace and provide His specific revelation for ongoing godly living.

I think, however, I was so enamored with these heroes that I didn't understand there were other heroes who added to their work by understanding God's revealing work in history and culture. There are dangers in syncretism, but there are also dangers of assuming that when we arrive, God arrives with us. I needed to add to my ability to see God in Scripture another set of eyes to see God in history and culture. I have a high view of Scripture and I do not believe these new eyes should change the picture laid down by Scripture. But these new eyes do add the ability to add high definition to the picture Scripture has already provided. More importantly, these new eyes allow me to understand that *my* contribution is less than I thought before, and to consider that God is much more active and powerful than what I had realized before.

For Christians, we believe what we are seeking to "see" is the Person who created us. Out of love for us, God has proactively revealed Himself to us through four increasingly explicit means:

General Revelation (both nature and the creation of the creatures made in God's image: that is cultures, relationships, events, circumstances, science, and art).

> *"For since the creation of the world God's invisible qualities—his eternal power and divine nature—have been clearly seen, being understood from what has been made, so that men are without excuse"*
>
> —ROMANS 1:20

Church History, Tradition, and Leaders. God has confirmed critical doctrinal issues through creeds, confessions, key events in history, and current church authorities. While these authorities are fallible and often have limited application to specific time and places in history, they often are validated by time and the continued witness of many godly leaders.

Specific Revelation (Scripture, inspired through specific writers and historical events).

> *"All Scripture is God-breathed and is useful for teaching, rebuking, correcting and training in righteousness, so that the man of God may be thoroughly equipped for every good work"*
>
> —2 TIMOTHY 3:16–17

God personally revealed on earth (First as God incarnated in the man Jesus, then the Holy Spirit as the Spirit of Truth).

> *"When a man believes in me, he does not believe in me only, but in the one who sent me. When he looks at me, he sees the one who sent me"* (John 12:44–45). *"And I will ask the Father, and he will give you another Counselor to be with you forever—the Spirit of truth"* (John 14:16–17). *"I have much more to say to you, more than you*

can now bear. But when he, the Spirit of truth, comes, he will guide you into all truth"

—JOHN 16: 12–13

If we want to see God, we have to look through all four of these means of revelation—knowing that the Holy Spirit opens our eyes, Scripture is never contradicted, and Jesus is the central focus of God's self-disclosure. These four means of revelation are in a hierarchy of importance with the incarnation and Scriptures at the top, yet all four work together. To pursue any one without engaging the others will severely limit our ability to see God as He desires us to see Him.

Today we have more access to Scripture than ever before through multiple translations, commentaries, and archeological and historical information about the writers and their times. With the advent of globalization, the Internet, and the nations coming to our cities and its neighborhoods, we also have more access to God's general revelation in the history and cultures of the world. It is an amazing time to be a seeker of God.

ABCD

The ability to see where God has preceded us is important not only to our spiritual formation, but also to our effectiveness as urban ministers. During the 1960s and 1970s, the most prevalent approach to urban ministry started by assessing needs. The first step of this approach was to assess what the neighborhood lacked. Elaborate research tools were developed to identify housing, medical, nutrition, structural, and other missing elements that were blocking the ability for people to experience a healthy neighborhood.

The second step of this approach gathered urban ministry experts to develop a strategy of how to target resources toward what the research showed was missing in the neighborhood. It was assumed that the neighborhood itself had little to offer to the solution. It was thought that the main way a neighborhood could grow to health were if ideas, people, and resources were added from outside of the neighborhood with priority attention on the greatest areas of deficit in the neighborhood.

However, through the leadership of urban ministry practitioners such as Ray Bakke and others during the 1960s and 1970s, another approach to urban ministry developed that focused on the assets of the neighborhood rather than its deficits. Research into these new models by John Kretzmann and John McKnight categorized these emerging models into some common steps called Asset Based Community Development (ABCD). Some of the assumptions of this new model included:

(1) **Asset-Based.** It is more important to appreciate and mobilize individual and community talents, skills, and assets than to focus on problems and needs.

(2) **Community.** Long-term gains will be much greater if the solutions are community-driven by leaders inside the community rather than resource-driven by outside agencies. It is also assumed that community driven solutions may start off slower with fewer visible gains, but in the long term, the benefits far outweigh the loss of quick results.

(3) **Development.** The focus of the work is not short-term relief, but the development of ongoing economic, health, social, governmental, and sometimes spiritual solutions.

(4) **Social capital.** The assets of people and relationships are more important to community health than money and other resource capital.

(5) **Participation.** Participatory methods help residents own the process and results.

(6) **Collaboration.** These methods are important to include a large number of community residents.

(7) **Civil Society.** It is important to help residents increasingly see their identity not as welfare recipients, but as citizens whose input and advocacy are important to make local government more effective and responsive.

A summary of how this approach works includes:

(1) **Research the assets of the community**—where health is already present that can be built on. One approach is called Appreciative Inquiry where neighborhood residents tell stories of good things that have happened in their neighborhood. For use in a larger, city-wide dialogue, Ray Bakke developed a method called the "Signs of Hope Consultation" in 1980, For three to five days, key government, business, community, education, and church leaders of a city meet to talk about best practices and outcomes in their city. In both methods, residents gain confidence in themselves and their ability to move forward in leading solutions from within the community.

(2) **Organize a core group of community leaders.** Often the stories in step one reveal people who are already recognized as leaders within the community and who have a passion to do something to improve their own neighborhood.

(3) **Map the assets in the community**—individuals, associations, and local institutions. The result is a better picture of what skills the individuals in the community possess; where there are both formal and informal relationships that are working well inside the community; and what relationships have already been naturally built with outside agencies. It is important that the mapping is done by the community residents themselves rather than outside experts. The map will identify the assets that exist within:

(a) Relationships and associations—what groups already exist

(b) Individual skills, talents, knowledge, and capacity

(c) Local institutions, businesses, and organizations

(d) Physical assets and natural resources

(e) Local economic networks, existing products, and potential products and services

(4) **Building a community vision and plan**—developed with participation and collaboration among community residents; sometimes facilitated by, but not dictated by outside agencies. Often what emerges is a development theme or a starter project that can be used to collect and focus the first stage of community leaders.

(5) **Mobilizing and linking neighborhood assets**—often the slow, persistent work of developing trust between factions within the neighborhood through small beginning projects and events. Over time, larger grassroots visions emerge from small successes and gain widespread acceptance. Trusted leaders begin to emerge and are given authority by the community. The level of ownership and connection between factions and groups increases. This is often a multi-year process and it is important that it is not rushed by impatience or a flood of resources from outside the community.

(6) **Facilitating and leveraging outside resources**—helping to direct volunteers, expertise, financial investments and donations, and other resources that are offered to the community from the outside. External resources are not accessed until local resources have been used. This puts the community in a position of strength in dealing with outside institutions.

Marriage of Good Practice and Good Formation

James 1:19 reads, "My dear brothers, take note of this: Everyone should be quick to listen, slow to speak. . . . " Most spiritual formation traditions place a higher priority on the disciplines of listening, silence and service, than on the practice of talking. For most of us, listening is harder than talking because it forces us to submit to someone else's agenda for a time. Silence is difficult because it stops our obsession with self-expression and forces us to listen. Service is often challenging because it means that not only do we listen to someone else's agenda, but we actually use our energy to serve that agenda.

It is much easier to serve someone who genuinely needs our help when we can also decide how they should be served. It is a test of patience, faith, and character to serve someone with less knowledge, experience, and expertise and have to submit to how they want us to serve them. It feels like driving down the street, aiming for every red light and pothole we can possibly find. It would be so much faster and feel so much better if we drove the car ourselves. It is frustrating to watch others make what feels to us like the wrong decisions, over and over again. It is even more frustrating when their decisions result in us having to expend our energy and resources in activities that feel futile, ineffective, and inefficient to us. One of the most frustrating disciplines of spiritual formation is silence and submission when you know that you have the answer and the capacity to provide the solution.

In 1990, Henry Blackaby wrote a popular book called *Experiencing God: Knowing and Doing the Will of God*. One of the central spiritual formation premises of the book is that we must discover where God is at work and join Him there. It is hard enough to put aside our agenda to join God's agenda. It is even harder when God's agenda is revealed through someone else that we perceive is less intelligent, less spiritual, or less experienced than ourselves. What may surprise us is that discerning where God is at work may not come from our disciplined quiet times, or skillful Bible study, or even from our logical assessments. It often comes from the places where we are least open to listen for it.

The key to spiritual formation is to discern God's work and join Him in that work. In story after story in Scripture, and in story after story in our lives, we often find God at work in the least likely places.

Foolish Things Make Us Feel Like Fools

"But God chose the foolish things of the world to shame the wise; God chose the weak things of the world to shame the strong. He chose the lowly things of this world and the despised things—and the things that are not—to nullify the things that are, so that no one may boast before him."

—1 CORINTHIANS 1:27–29

The passage applies directly to the work of Jesus Christ on the Cross and salvation that is not earned but freely given. But it also indirectly applies to how God often chooses the least likely *people* to accomplish the greatest things for Him. One of the great spiritual opportunities of urban ministry is the blessing of having to submit to people who seem to be worse leaders than ourselves; to face the anger of our hearts as we serve in futility. Then slowly, we learn how God requires us to disconnect our core identity from our money, skills, capacity, and time in order to then use these things to serve Him well.

So as we are shamed by our dependence on ourselves, we become more dependent upon God. We also discover that some of the people we thought were foolish, inexperienced, and ineffective, God reveals to be urban geniuses and great leaders. Often it was hidden from us at first because most of us assume at some level that circumstances of poverty are caused by lack of intelligence, ability, or discipline. Our biases make it hard to see the genius of leaders who are poor. As we stop constantly selling our ideas, sometimes we are amazed at how better ideas are emerging from very unlikely people.

Yet, often the reason we are surprised by the genius of community leaders is because we have blessed and equipped them and they have finally had an opportunity to flourish in ways God always intended. Our role is to serve their agenda, but our role is also to bless them with our presence, words, help, and love.

Review

The key to effective urban ministry is to arrive with open ears and eyes and look for how God has prepared the people and the place for what He intends. When we arrive with eyes that see only needs that exist, problems that must be fixed, and how we can exert our ideas and influence, we will not be able to see how God has preceded us.

Asset-based community development is both an effective urban ministry practice and an effective practice for spiritual formation. The practice provides confidence and empowerment to urban leaders who will continue to live in the community and continue to build the long-term solutions. ABCD builds humility among those who want to assist them from outside of the community. Yet, even beyond that, ABCD reflects a knowledge of God—that He is already present in a neighborhood long before we arrive.

■ ■ ■ Personal Reflection

Where have you seen God's work in your life when it was very obvious that you joined something that He was already doing and you could not take personal credit for the results?

Where do you most often learn about where God is working around you?

Do you have any sources of learning about God's work that would be hard for you to receive?

If not, do you think you have turned off your ears to any of those sources of discernment in your life?

■ ■ ■ Bible Reflection

Read Romans 1:18–25 and Hebrews 11:1–13. For some, these verses seem to indicate God revealed His character enough through sources other than Scriptures so that some could be prepared to receive Him and eternal salvation in Jesus Christ.

How do you feel about God's justice and love for "pagan" or "unreached" cultures?

How does this both increase your urgency to tell people about the work of Christ revealed in Scriptures, but also release you from a false burden of thinking their response depends on your ability to present it perfectly?

Read Ephesians 2:6–10. What do you think it means that we are "God's workmanship, created in Christ Jesus to do good works, which God prepared in advance for us to do"?

Chapter Five: WORKING WITH FIRE

Spiritual Formation Principle #5: God calls us to steward money and power as we serve the poor and the powerful in the city.

Theme: Urban ministry continues to center on relief and development activities, but is prioritizing advocacy for the poor increasingly.

Bible Reading:
Genesis 1:26–30; 2:19–20
1 John 2:15-17

In the 1980s, I was trained in the traditional approaches to urban ministry. I often heard this metaphor, "If you give a person a fish, they will eat for a day. If you teach a person to fish, they will eat for a lifetime." By the late eighties, most urban leaders realized that the urban world was full of broken and evil systems that urban ministry based only on social services and education didn't adequately address. These leaders were frustrated that, as fast as they met needs and trained leaders, these evil systems would create more needs and invalidate the new leaders. The metaphor was extended by questions such as:

"But what if the pond is zoned to not allow people of your race to fish there?"

"But what if there is fence around the pond so it can be developed into a golf course?"

"But what if the pond is so polluted that the fish cannot be eaten?"

These questions have caused the focus of urban ministry to change quickly. Today, urban ministry usually incorporates three major areas of study:

(1) Relief—meeting the immediate needs of people

(2) Development—building ongoing systems for health

(3) Advocacy—changing the laws and systems of evil that are prevalent in the city

Sometimes a firefighting metaphor is used to show the relationship between these three. Relief is like *fighting fires.* You go to where there are fires and focus only on putting them out. But after awhile you realize, though some fires are unique, many fires are reoccurring in the exact same places and in the same ways. So *development* involves building *fire prevention systems* such as sprinkler systems, fire barriers, and in educating people on safe practices in the places where fires reoccur. Yet even so, some buildings are built with highly flammable materials or have inadequate fire escapes. So *advocacy* is like *changing the fire codes and improving their enforcement* so that the fire prevention systems are more effective and there are fewer fires to fight.

Urban ministries today not only provide more relief activities, but increasing amounts of development and advocacy activities. For example, Ray Bakke provides examples about the role of politics, power, and race in Chicago history. As a result, in Chicago and every other city, there are many examples of evil and unjust systems that stymie the most sophisticated community development efforts. Because of this, advocacy has become the front edge of new urban ministry innovations.

Advocacy: From Revolution to Collaboration

For most of the 20th century, the dominant advocacy model emerged from the work of Saul Alinsky and the Industrial Areas Foundation he founded. The model was formed in the 1930s as Alinsky organized revolts against horrid working conditions in Chicago's Union Stockyards. By the 1960s, the foundation had widespread influence among community organizers in almost every major US city. Some credit Alinsky with developing new approaches to politics; using tactics that allowed the poor and disenfranchised to fight city hall effectively.

Using media, political, and economic pressure, Alinsky saw many successes in improving how city systems serve the poor. His model thrived on tactics to help the poor understand themselves as victims, to embolden people to lash out against their victimizers, and to embarrass the elite power-holders unresponsive to the needs of the poor. Donna Schaper writes, in "A Rakes Progress":

> "Alinsky thought of himself as a radical . . . He personified the American theory of pragmatism in his commitment to power: 'Whatever works to get power to the people, use it.' That didn't mean violence but rather serious attention to matters of power. Pack the meeting. Fill the streets. Flood the office with post cards. If that doesn't work, find something that does, including humor."
>
> "At one point to gain attention from the Chicago city council, Alinsky threatened to flush all the toilets at O'Hare airport at once. Before the toilet flushing escapade ever had a chance to happen, the city council gave in and granted some demands. Another time, in Rochester, New York, Alinsky had a fart-in at the Eastman Kodak Board meeting. A baked bean supper had been organized for participants."

One of the primary assumptions of the Alinsky model was that power was held by a few elite city leaders and the primary means to change unjust systems was to create a grassroots revolt against the elite.

However, the power structure of US cities started to change drastically in the late 1960s and throughout the 1970s and early 1980s. Starting with Carl Stokes in Cleveland in 1967, then Tom Bradley in Los Angeles in 1973, and Maynard Jackson in Atlanta in 1974, African-American leaders were elected as mayors, signaling a significant political shift in large US cities. Before this, most cities were run by a small group of Anglo male business leaders who, in some cases, ruled over the city as benevolent caretakers, and in other cases widely abused their power. Most cities still have freeways, parks, major streets, and civic buildings named after long-forgotten individuals who served in this role. Yet, as "white flight" to the suburbs decimated these leaders' power base, a much more decentralized system of power—divided between mayors, city councils, city managers, and local representatives—often replaced those power brokers..

With new power structures, the key obstacle was no longer the insensitivity of a small group of elite power holders. Now there was a myriad of political leaders, all representing their particular segment of the city, fighting against each other to gain enough power through quickly shifting coalitions to focus resources on their districts. The old model of attacking city hall quickly became ineffective as "city hall" was often in constant civil war and an outside attack simply added another obstacle to the struggle to create enough coalition power to effect positive change.

Bakke Graduate University board member Janet Morrow was one of the first people to recognize this shift. In 1971, Morrow created among Chicago city leaders a peer-learning organization called TRUST, Inc. (To Reshape Urban Systems Together). Dubbed an urban policy think-tank, TRUST provided a peer forum for cross-interest group communication and cooperative problem solving. Instead of Alinsky-style grassroots activism that had attacked a centralized power base on behalf of the poor, this new approach served as a somewhat neutral outside convener that provided the glue to align competing interests in order to serve the poor. Since the power was no longer held just within city hall, TRUST change strategies linked Chicago government, business, church, community, and education leaders. The results included new state legislation, a constitutional amendment passed by Illinois voters and major policy changes in city and state departments, and public and private foundation funding priorities. Again, Chicago birthed a new model for city transformation efforts that has influenced every other large US city for four decades since.

Spiritual Formation: From Separatism to Stewardship

As urban ministry has increased its emphasis on advocacy, Christian spiritual formation also has gone through major changes. During the mid-1980s, I was hired to research, develop, and implement a school-wide spiritual formation program in a seminary with more than 1,500 students. During that time, spiritual formation was defined mostly as:

(1) Spiritual disciplines—with the greatest emphasis on private, reflective disciplines such as prayer, Bible reading, meditation, silence, journaling, reading devotional literature

(2) One-on-one counseling—often called "spiritual direction" in regular meetings where one person led another through an exploration of motives, feelings, attitudes, and behavior.

These two emphases are the foundation on which most spiritual formation models are built. Spiritual disciplines are nonnegotiable, fundamental practices of spiritual formation. Many writers use the terms *Spiritual Formation* and *Contemplative Spirituality* as though they are synonymous. During my early exposure to the themes of spiritual formation, I spent much time learning and practicing a host of contemplative practices. I did prayer and solitude retreats in local monasteries, and read the rich devotional writings of amazing Christian contemplatives from past centuries. I was trained as a spiritual director and took on extra counseling training to hone skills in exploring the depths of my own heart motivations and to guide the same search in others.

Yet, the more I explored the realm of spiritual formation, the more I realized it was dominated by writers and speakers who are naturally gifted reflectors and teachers. Many are gifted with identifiably passive, calm personalities known as Type B personalities, and can spend long hours in solitude to reflect on God's character and the motives of their hearts. At first I felt that my action-oriented personality meant something was wrong with me and I needed to discipline myself to change to become more sedate. There is much in the spiritual formation literature that illustrates in detail how Type-A people run roughshod over Type-B people and miss God's best gifts by being too active and too shallow to reflect on their heart motives. These observations are true mostly, and it is a powerful experience to have someone with a very different personality point out the darker side of your own. Yet, over time, I considered that, maybe, the spiritual formation field definitions excluded activities and people God intended to include.

During my research from then to now, I have rarely seen the terms *urban ministry* and *spiritual formation* used together. Urban ministry types often are "ready, aim, fire" people. We jump in with both feet to meet needs, develop solutions, and fight injustice. We are busy, engaged people who often experience God more so in service than in meditation.

In spite of what it may at first seem, spiritual formation should not exclude the natural gifts of active, engaged personalities. Spiritual formation means our active involvement in the process God uses to form us spiritually. Often our active involvement includes exploring heart motives—digging deep to discover increasing levels of sin and rebellion hidden from us, recognizing that the Holy Spirit is the initiator and sustainer of our spiritual growth. But this formation also recognizes that we play a part in either resisting or cooperating with the work the Holy Spirit does in our life. If we assume that the Holy Spirit speaks the loudest in quiet, withdrawn places, then certainly those of us who are wired by God from birth to be active and engaged have a severe disadvantage. Jesus retreated at key times to pray. But most of what is written about Jesus in the gospels shows an active, engaged Christ. We somehow have bought the notion that Jesus filled His spiritual tanks when He was alone and then depleted those tanks when He was active and engaged. Actually, he was always "spiritually full." Jesus kept His spiritual tanks filled in different ways, when He withdrew and when He engaged others. He is our premier example. For me, this means that I need to pursue a spiritual formation that occurs in quiet places *and* noisy city streets, and in times of rest *and* times of work.

I think it is a mistake to buy the commonly held idea that the only way we can explore heart motives is through contemplative disciplines, spiritual directors, and finding obscure 16th-century quotes from Teresa of Avila. Urban ministry types tend to be streetwise to others' motives and blunt in expressing what they see. We don't worry much about offending others. What deep insights we lack in not having contemplative personalities, we often gain through the insults of our homeboys. We have the opportunity to gain much as we allow our community to speak truth into what *they* see about our motives. Our approach may be crude and no one's going to slow down to take the time to write it up prettily, but urban ministry is an ideal place for intense spiritual formation.

In chapter 9, we'll look more into this world of action-oriented spiritual formation and focus on spiritual formation that is practiced in the midst of stewarding the big three: power, money and sex. The starting place is to understand that spiritual formation is not a way to avoid these things. Greater trust and dependence upon God reveals His purpose for us, which propels us to move headlong into stewarding these three well.

Earth Governors

Genesis 1:28 is often called "the cultural mandate." It includes the first-recorded words that God says to humans. It reads, *"God blessed them and said to them, 'Be fruitful and increase in number; fill the earth and subdue it. Rule over the fish of the sea and the birds of the air and over every living creature that moves on the ground.'"* In Genesis 1, God has created earth and all kinds of creatures on earth. He creates one special creature who will act as his governor (traditional theology calls this His "Vice Regent"). Verse 28 is God giving this creature the purpose for his existence.

Also, this passage hints at what type of tools God has given to His new governors. The first one is human sexuality. God made humans as male and female. Sex is the way they will increase in number. Sex is something they must steward well in order to accomplish their purpose. The second tool is power. *Subduing* means using power to put things into order. Ruling requires exerting authority and influence over those who are to be ruled.

The last tool is not so obvious and is an extension of power. Granted, to arrive at this tool is a bit of a rabbit trail, but it will prove important later in this chapter. If Adam and Eve had not eaten the fruit in Genesis 3, then more and more people would have been born, but without fallen natures. I believe that they would have organized themselves into groups to accomplish various aspects of ruling the earth. Each one would have had different gifts. Some might have had sowing gifts, and they would be the sowers of the group. Others would have been trimmers and harvesters. If one group produced only wheat, they would have approached another group that produced only rice and asked if they could trade some wheat for rice.

What would you call an organization that utilizes people's God-given gifts for the purpose of producing something of value that can be traded to another organization doing the same? I think a good word for this is *business*. Granted, this is not the modern Wall Street definition that includes a concept that only emerged about 50 years ago called "maximizing profits." But if the population of the Garden had grown to be thousands, millions, or billions, many of us would be subduing our earth using the tool of business. If there were no moral evil, then we might not need the institution called government. If God walked with us in the cool of the day, then we might not need the institution called church. But we would need the institutions called the family and business. It is interesting to think about our current jobs and which of our careers would not be needed if we were still in the Garden.

However, as this Garden society grew, there would be some products such as rubber that could only be produced in equatorial climates, and other products such as maple syrup that could only be produced in colder climates. To facilitate the efficient trading between these "Garden businesses," we would have to create a currency. Then we'd find ourselves using money, which is an extension of power, even in the Garden. So we would be the governors of the world, ruling the world through sex, power, and money.

Genesis 2 retells the story of Genesis 1 from a different camera angle, a common way stories were told in very ancient times. This angle gives us the detail of Adam naming all the animals in Genesis 2:19–20. God never interrupts or corrects. He lets His governor confirm his authority over the created animals by naming them. It is a passing of the baton from the Creator who still owns these animals to His steward who would manage these animals on behalf of the owner. It is not a sale. The Creator still retains ownership. It is not making Adam and Eve slaves. They don't simply take and follow orders. Adam and Eve are given authority to make independent decisions about these animals. As stewards, their "boss" tells them the general direction of what He wants and then they figure out the details. They always have the understanding that their decisions must please the owner of Creation. They were created to work for Him and if they ever get separated from Him, their whole purpose and their joy are lost.

They are a lamp that looks good on the table, but only works when plugged into the electrical socket. They are hardware that just sits there blinking unless someone loads in software. They are a cell phone that turns on and looks nice but requires a SIM card to connect to a network to make calls. The point of their existence is to be connected to their Creator as stewards over His creation.

However, in Genesis 3, they disconnect. They decide that perhaps the electrical plug is holding them back; the software will not think of their best interest; the SIM card will control them in ways they are not free to decide what is best for them on their own.

The first two chapters of the Bible show us what humans are like when they are fully plugged into God. We live in a garden. The last two chapters of the Bible show us what we are like when we are fully plugged in again. We live in a city called New Jerusalem. The rest of the Bible shows us what happens when we are unplugged. We are only shadows of what we were intended to be—billions of lamps sitting on tables, in the dark, not able to be turned on to illuminate the beauty of our lampshade or the room. Over time, we begin to believe that our purpose is to sit in the dark. Lamps are pole-like creatures with long cord-like tails with two prongs on the end and wide-brim hats. Our purpose is to be in dark rooms doing the best we can to be happy there.

However, Romans 8 shows us a surprise even in the midst of the large section of time between the Garden and New Jerusalem.

"Because those who are led by the Spirit of God are sons of God. For you did not receive a spirit that makes you a slave again to fear, but

you received the Spirit of sonship. And by him we cry, 'Abba, Father.' The Spirit himself testifies with our spirit that we are God's children. Now if we are children, then we are heirs—heirs of God and co-heirs with Christ, if indeed we share in his sufferings in order that we may also share in his glory. I consider that our present sufferings are not worth comparing with the glory that will be revealed in us. The creation waits in eager expectation for the sons of God to be revealed. For the creation was subjected to frustration, not by its own choice, but by the will of the one who subjected it, in hope that the creation itself will be liberated from its bondage to decay and brought into the glorious freedom of the children of God. We know that the whole creation has been groaning as in the pains of childbirth right up to the present time. Not only so, but we ourselves, who have the first fruits of the Spirit, groan inwardly as we wait eagerly for our adoption as sons, the redemption of our bodies. For in this hope we were saved."

—ROMANS 8:14–24A

This passage shows that there are some lamps in those dark rooms that have been plugged back into the wall socket. Some people have been reconnected and they are the new Adams and Eves of the world. Their electrical cords are frayed and their shades are covered with dust so they give off the wavering glow rather than a bright light. But the light is enough to show the other lamps that the room they are in was made to have light, and they have a purpose beyond just sitting on a table in the dark. Some of the lamps are upset at the other lamps for showing them that another greater purpose exists. Others wish they could do the same but are not willing to plug in. Yet others are thrilled to learn that what they have dreamed of their whole lives can be reality. The other objects in the room groan, waiting for the lamps to get new cords and clean lamp shades so they can realize their full purpose too.

That passage in Romans talks about Christians as being God's children again—as Adam and Eve were. We can call God "Abba" or "Daddy"—just like Adam and Eve did. And while all humans are born to be governors of the earth, we are the only ones who are reconnected to the King who appointed us to this position; sort of like Adam and Eve were. Our connection at this point is in part. We taste the electricity but know that it falls short of what it should be and someday will be. We taste our created purpose just enough to give us hope, but not enough to finally satisfy us.

As the only governors who are plugged into the King, we have a different responsibility than the other governors who are not plugged in. We have a calling to steward the world and, in doing so, to demonstrate the positive advantages of what other governors could experience if they plugged in. This is what some people call the Great Commission—to tell people of our purpose to be plugged in, the future benefits of this in eternity, and the present benefits in part on this earth.

The label "Great Commission" that was placed on Matthew 28:18–20 in the 19th century is a bit of a misnomer. It makes it appear as if the first commission of Genesis 1:28 is the "Not So Great Commission" or perhaps the "OK Commission." Yet, if we have to create marketing slogans for Bible passages, then a more accurate label would be that Genesis 1:28 is the "Original Commission," and Matthew 28 is the "Continued Commission." The point being that the two are connected. The "Second Commission" of Matthew 28 is a restatement in the fallen world of what the "First Commission" in Genesis 1 stated in the non-fallen world.

Matthew 28:20 says, *"teaching them to obey all that I commanded you."* If you look earlier in the Book of Matthew, Jesus uses the word "kingdom" 53 times in that book alone. *Kingdom* is a word that describes what it looks like when God's governors are in their places, connected and obedient to the King. Jesus's teaching described the kingdom from many different camera angles. Jesus's life displays fully what a true governor looks like among fallen governors. He was fully God, but He was also fully submissive to His Father as an example of how a human governor should be fully submissive to the King who appointed Him. Jesus died to provide a way for us to reconnect to God as His governors in part on this earth, and in full in the New Jerusalem in heaven. The Kingdom is now among us partially. As theologians describe it, "Already, but not yet."

When Jesus says, "Teach them all that I commanded you," we'd have to do some painful and complicated gymnastics to take the concept of the kingdom out of a curriculum that included "all." In essence, the "Second Commission" is a commission to teach the "First Commission" so well that people want to accept Jesus as their Savior and reconnect to their God-created purpose on earth and for eternity.

Toddlers Driving Ferraris

So here we sit, untrained governors with a high horsepower set of tools. We are like babies given laser guns called money, sex, and power. It is not surprising that we are scared to use these things. Most of us have been taught that what God really wants us to do is to put down the laser guns, go hide away from other people who are using them very poorly, do evangelism to grab a few to come with us, and then wait for Jesus to return with a sword in His mouth.

When I was growing up, the Bible passage that was used to justify this plan was 1 John 2:15–17, which reads,

> *Do not love the world or anything in the world. If anyone loves the world, the love of the Father is not in him. For everything in the world—the cravings of sinful man, the lust of his eyes and the boasting of what he has and does—comes not from the Father but from the world. The world and its desires pass away, but the man who does the will of God lives forever.*

I was told the phrase "cravings of sinful man" was supposed to be sexual lust; the "lust of his eyes" was materialistic greed; and boasting of what he has and does was desire for power and fame. As a shortcut, it came out that we should basically avoid sex, money, and power. But the shortcut changed the whole meaning of the verse.

I'm not the only one that got this message growing up. In class notes, I often include a sentence that says, "According to 1 Timothy 6:10, the root of all evil is _____." Well over 70 percent of students will fill the blank with the word *money* (granted, it is only one blank, which makes people assume I am looking for one word). The actual answer is "the *love of* money." This makes a big difference in how we view money. The wrong answer says money is inherently evil. The right answer says that money is neutral, but the love of it is evil.

God gave us sex, money, and power to steward. Yes, these are dangerous things to steward and we see the whole world obsessed with them. But as we fear them, we abdicate our stewardship of them. And what happens when we who are called to steward abdicate our role? Hollywood took on the task to steward how the world should view sex; Wall Street took on the task of how we should steward money; and Washington, D.C., took over the task of how we should steward power. These are unconnected governors and they haven't done the job very well, but how could they if they are disconnected from the Creator of these things?

When another steward is scared of his assignment in Matthew 25 and buries the talents his king gives to him, the king calls him, "You wicked, lazy servant" (v. 26). Stewardship of money, power, and sex is a dangerous, but necessary job for any Christian. This is especially true for Christians serving the least, the last, and the lost; those who have been most abused by the world's obsession and poor management of these things. Some people have described Bakke Graduate University as a whole doctoral program committed to creating peer learning among the most advanced urban leaders of the world, to study how to do this. Even then, we feel we have barely scratched the surface of this too-often-ignored topic. The purpose of this chapter is to introduce the idea that for urban ministers to be effective advocates, they must be in a lifelong journey in a community of other Christians, to learn how to steward money, sexuality, and power well for the welfare of the world, and for the least, the last, and the lost.

■ ■ ■ Personal Reflection

In which of the areas of comprehensive urban ministry—that includes relief, development, and advocacy—have you had the most and least training and experience?

Have you ever been exposed to a religious subculture of separatism? How did that prepare you or distracts you from being a steward of money, power, and sexuality?

■ ■ ■ Bible Reflection

Read Genesis 1:26–30; 2:19–20

What are the specific instructions that God gave to Adam and Eve?

According to this passage, about what areas of their work does God not give them instruction?

Read 1 John 2:15–17

How is "the world" defined in this passage? What aspects of our life and culture are things we should *not* love, and what aspects of our life and culture should we love?

Chapter Six: GIVE AWAY RIGHTS

Spiritual Formation Principle #6: God calls us to give away our personal right to make decisions—even if we think we know best.

Theme: Urban ministry is more about empowerment than it is about money, solutions, or even concrete progress. Understanding past mistakes will make all the difference in how we do urban ministry today.

Bible Reading:
Genesis 2:19–20
Matthew 5:1–10; 6:1–4

Lessons Learned from War

On January 8, 1964, US President Lyndon Johnson announced in his State of the Union speech legislation for a War on Poverty to address a national poverty rate of almost 19 percent. The War on Poverty speech led Congress to pass the Economic Opportunity Act, opening up a variety of new initiatives to bring new government resources to distressed economic areas.

In contrast in 1996, the US Congress passed the Personal Responsibility and Work Opportunity Reconciliation Act, whose purpose as articulated by President Bill Clinton was to "end welfare as we know it." By the time the 1996 laws were signed, many of the enormous housing projects built during the War on Poverty had become seedbeds of even greater crime and social problems than the ghettos that had preceded them. Most were either torn down or in the process of being vacated in order to be demolished. Many of the direct welfare programs established in the mid-1960s had either been eradicated or drastically changed to promote "personal responsibility." Only a few programs such as the Job Corps or the Head Start program, which emphasized empowering people to take their own destiny in hand, survived the massive shift in national welfare policy.

What happened between 1964 and 1996 that created almost opposite approaches to addressing poverty in the US? The reasons are hotly debated. Some historians quote statistics to prove that the War on Poverty was successful and, therefore, the 1996 laws were built on the successful foundation laid by the previous approach. Some claim the two-term presidency of Ronald Reagan ended the War on Poverty before the full positive effects could be realized. Others claim the War on Poverty vastly contributed to the breakdown of the African-American family by creating incentives for single mothers not to get married and to remain unemployed. Critics point out that housing projects intensified ghettos and isolated the poor from the rest of the city and from opportunities.

One of the few things that most people can agree on about the War on Poverty is that it demonstrated that welfare without empowerment does not provide long-term solutions. If people are given resources—but not the ability to choose how to use those resources—they may end up with better circumstances immediately but with a worse self-image. Over time, it takes greater and greater resources to shore up circumstantial gains as whole communities fall into greater despair. Providing better nutrition, clothing, or housing in ways that do not allow people to be proud of themselves or to feel in control of their own destiny ultimately creates greater despair. There is something about the way humans are made that causes us to thrive when we are given the ability to make decisions that affect our circumstances.

For urban ministry to be successful, we must be more effective at giving away decisions, power, and knowledge than in giving away money, medicine, housing, and food. But there are innate desires in all of us that make it easier for us to give away resources than it is for us to give away power and to facilitate dignity.

Fix-It Heroes

When my youngest son was a 7-year-old, my wife and I discovered that a trip to the dollar store to buy a cheap plastic toy could be as satisfying to him as buying something that requires batteries and costs 20 times more. It was amazing how a trip to the dollar store could motivate him. Toys got put away. Table set. Dishwasher emptied. Chores accomplished. Contrary to the findings of modern science, a seven-year-old boy *can* focus with the right motivation. Bribery remained alive and well in our family so he had quite a collection of cheap plastic toys.

As a result, I also had an in-box in the kitchen where he put his cheap plastic toys when they broke. Almost daily, I would find a truck with a tire broken off, a sword with a broken tip, or an airplane with a wing dislocated. In a drawer nearby: dad's secret fix-it weapon—a small bottle of super-adhesive with a pin-point dispenser.

There has been something amazingly satisfying about being able to fix a broken plastic toy and then deliver it to my son to watch his big grin. Just taking something broken and making it concretely better satisfies my soul deeply. I really want to be the fix-it hero. I realize that my time of fix-it bliss could last only a few years. Yet I reveled in fix-it bliss while it occurred. The time would come when he would come to me with broken adolescent relationships and hormone-driven anxieties.

In contrast, when my 10-year old son and my 11-year-old daughter passed the fix-it hero stage, I was not yet out of my league. They still had broken toys I could fix. But instead of asking me to fix things for them, they wanted me to show them how to fix things themselves. At first, it was frustrating to me because they didn't fix them as well as I could have. Super-strong adhesive is fairly unforgiving and once the parts are placed together crooked, they are crooked until the next time that toy breaks in the exact same spot. Having crooked toys around the house reflected on my fathering skills so this was hard to watch. Sometimes they would get very frustrated as they worked hard on fixing something and it did not turn out how they wanted. However, I only added to the frustration if I reminded them that I could have fixed it better. I came to realize that they would rather experience the frustration than avoid it by having me fix it for them.

As a result, I have found with the older children that their biggest smiles were when *they* fixed things, even if nowhere close to their dad's standards. They have rarely cared about perfection; mostly they have cared about fixing things themselves. It is amazing to watch how fast children want Dad to move from fix-it hero to background coach and cheerleader to their adventures.

There is a time for being the hero. There is a time for being the invisible coach. Being free to move from one role to the other and find joy in both roles is one of the most important spiritual formation journeys we can take.

Fix-It Futility at Home

Because each of us—especially males, I believe)—want to be fix-it heroes at some level, we tend to approach much of our work, ministry, and relationships as means to showcase our fix-it skills. The first place we learn our audience doesn't appreciate our great fix-it prowess is marriage. I recall the two solid pieces of advice I got at an engagement party:

(1) She doesn't want you to fix it. Even if you think you could fix it, she probably doesn't agree with you, so don't try. She just wants a hug.

(2) Don't argue. You will never win. Just say, "Yes, dear."

Oh, how I wish I had listened to this seasoned and timeless wisdom the first time. Even though the question may sound like, "I have this problem; can you fix it?" the real question is "Do you really love me?" Fixing something is much easier than demonstrating authentic love, but rarely satisfies to answer the real question.

Fix-it Futility at Work

After realizing that we will not be fix-it heroes at home, we then go forth hoping that we can be fix-it heroes at work. However, there we discover the logic-defying world of office politics. The best solution is rarely the one that wins the day. The better you prove beyond a doubt the superiority of your solution, the more likely it will be ignored. The harder you work on fixing problems, the more opportunity you give colleagues not working on solutions to schmooze with those who determine promotions.

After realizing that we will not be fix-it heroes at home or at work, then we look to another place to find "fix-it" fulfillment. My father-in-law, who spent much of the latter part of his life facilitating major corporate mergers and acquisitions, one day told me,

> "It is my experience that the nastiest fights occur after 5 p.m. (refer-ring to church and nonprofit work). When we buy out a company, we can give the existing management enough of a financial sev-erance that they can leave and keep their pride. Then we put in the right kind of new management and earn that severance back in the first three to six months. There is something about money that allows people to detach their personal identity from the job and objectively measure how well an idea performs over time. However, church and nonprofit boards don't have that luxury. People defend their idea as if their mother's honor, the future of the nation, and their very identity depended on their idea. And there are fewer objective means to determine the strength of the idea over time, so the argument continues on and on and on."

Some people take out their frustrations in their workplace by becoming bullies on nonprofit boards. It is human nature to seek out places where we can feel power-ful, significant, and influential. For many, it is tempting to see urban ministry as that place because it appears as if those to whom we are ministering are begging us to "fix it." Yet, in reality, they are actually asking us "Do you love me?" In many cases, the answer to the second question is not "Let me do it for you," but "How can I help you fix it—in your way, in your timing, so that you are the one who feels significant?"

The key to effective urban ministry goes back to constantly looking into our hearts to ask, *Why*? When we approach urban ministry as a means to make ourselves feel significant, we will want people to hear *our* strategies and ideas. When we approach urban ministry as a place to form us spiritually, we will want to listen to where God has preceded us and to join Him there.

Urban ministry that starts with "Let me tell you my idea," or "Let me show you what I can give to you," or "Let *me* do that for you" will be like watering your flowers with a liquid weed killer. For a short time, the plants will perk up as they absorb the water deep into their stems and root systems. But when you come out the next morning, they will be dead. Resources given to people without empowerment is poison. It will make them flourish for a season, but you have ultimately robbed them of yet another piece of their life-giving understanding of what it means to be made in the image of God.

Relationships or Strategies; Which Come First?

During the early 1990s, I was asked to facilitate several meetings between the pastors of the largest African-American churches and suburban business leaders in Dallas. The meetings picked up some positive press and were billed as a new innovation in creating citywide initiatives. Yet, being on the inside of the meetings, I realized that each meeting was cordial but not really exciting. The press releases afterward expressed great hope. But, in reality, we weren't accomplishing much and there was a great deal of public "face" on both sides—followed by private frustration.

The suburban leaders expressed their frustration that the urban leaders would show up late, tell stories, express a great deal of enthusiasm, and even agree on follow-up steps. But then they would rarely do the follow-up steps that they promised and were often hard to reach in between meetings.

The urban leaders expressed their frustration that the suburban leaders would show up with detailed plans and strategies already in mind. They would talk about how much money they were willing to put into *their* strategies. They pushed hard for others to agree to their next steps in their strategies. These pastors knew their communities. Some had relationships that went back several generations. Some of the suburban strategies were not bad, but these pastors knew in their gut that something wasn't safe and it would be damaging for these strategies and accompanying resources to descend on their people.

Over time, these meetings, like others in so many other cities, eventually simply faded away. The suburban leaders were busy. They were used to approaching projects with the question, "If we can decide on an effective strategy, *then* I'll invest time into building the relationships." The urban leaders were busy. They were used to approaching projects with the question, "If we develop the relationships, *then* I'll invest time into working on the strategies." Like ships passing unseen in the night, these two groups of leaders missed the opportunity to do a tremendous work for the city because they had two different languages of commitment and trust.

I learned from this experience that the greatest generosity that suburban leaders can give is their time and presence. Leaders from outside of the neighborhood must put their strategies on the altar for God to take away and never use if it is His will, and to not take credit for them if God *does* decide to use them. Urban leaders need the resources, but they can't accept them if the strings attached will be more harmful than the good the resources bring.

Larry James, who runs a ministry in Dallas that includes a large food bank, has a crisp way of making this point. Early in his ministry, he started displacing suburban volunteers by paying people in the immediate neighborhood to do the front-line food-bank jobs. Some of the suburban leaders complained that this would greatly increase the amount of food that was stolen. Larry replied, "Yes, it is true that in this business there is theft. But I would rather have people steal cans of corn than have people steal human dignity."

It is often hard for an urban leader to say this directly. People who live in poor neighborhoods are acutely aware that volunteers from outside can leave any time they want to and never come back. It often creates hard choices; "Do I tell them the truth that their ideas and superior attitude are harmful, or do I play up to them so I can get some help?" As a result, it may feel to a suburban leader as though these urban leaders are expressing enthusiasm but sabotaging progress. The temptation for suburban leaders then is to do the following:

(a) Leave and look for another place of ministry where their ideas are appreciated and they get the good "front-line" jobs or public kudos.

(b) Play urban leaders off one another until they find one who will implement suburban leaders' ideas.

(c) Exaggerate the scale of the project and money involved until urban leaders can't afford not to give attention to their ideas.

(d) Give money without time and presence and settle into a comfortable but distant transactional relationship.

The temptation for urban leaders is to continue to express enthusiasm to these suburban leaders to keep them in the game, but never hand over to them the power of relationships, connection, and access that would be necessary for them to be effective in the city. Because of a long track-record of short-term heroes who come in with big promises and leave when they don't get their way, urban leaders can get into a habit of viewing suburban leaders as temporary resource providers. They assume suburban leaders probably won't stay in the relationship for the long haul, but can supply resources until becoming disillusioned and then, disappear. The game is to get what you can before they eventually leave.

Many urban leaders feel they are in a constant survival mode—keeping their heads just above the financial and emotional waters. These short-term, transactional visitors from the suburbs with big dreams are one of the sources of keeping urban leaders afloat financially. Dashed hopes can be expensive financially and emotionally. It is hard to have the energy to act beyond the mode of surviving one more day.

So what happens too often is that relationships are broken, trust is diminished, and both urban and suburban leaders walk away with a wariness toward urban-suburban partnerships. In most cases, there is adequate supply of resources but an overabundance of ego on both sides so the solutions hoped for are never realized.

Giving Away Power

Ray Bakke's brother Dennis wrote a book in 2006 called *Joy at Work* that reached number eight on the *New York Times* Business Best Sellers list. The book tells the story of the Applied Energy Services (AES), which at one point supplied 100 million people with energy, often in developing nations. After Russia and France, the company was the largest owner of electrical power. At its peak, AES had 40,000 employees in 36 nations around the world.

Dennis cofounded AES in the 1980s. It became famous in the early 1990s for stating that its purpose was not profit-maximization but to provide safe, clean, reliable electricity. The SEC put a warning on its initial public offering, stating that AES had an unusual view of the purpose of business and it was not planning to change the values it had as a private corporation when it added public shareholders. Later, the company was in the headlines again for calculating how much carbon dioxide it was producing by coal-fired plants in the northern hemisphere. Applied Energy Services then bought thousands of acres of southern hemisphere forestlands and planted millions of trees that turned carbon dioxide back into oxygen.

Most people assumed that when Dennis wrote a book about his company, the book would focus on AES as being arguably the largest company in recent years that had a clear purpose and practice that placed social good above profits.

Yet, only chapter 7 of the book discusses this directly. The rest of the book has one dominant theme throughout; for top corporate leaders to do the right thing, they should give away decision-making authority to as many people in the company as possible. Joy in work comes from being able to personally make the decisions that control your circumstances. One of the most important things a CEO can do is to *not* make all the decisions, and to establish values and structures that give away to decisions to the people most affected by those decisions. For Dennis, the most important contribution of the company was not the trees, the unusual purpose, or even supplying so many developing nations with reliable electricity; it was to treat so many employees in a way that reflected they had been made in the image of God and were capable of making decisions.

Dennis's book explains why AES did not have a centralized human resources department or other large departments common in most large multinational corporations' headquarters. It was assumed that each plant worker would dedicate 80 percent of time to line functions such as running the plant, and 20 percent to localized staff functions, such as human resources, investing the financial capital of the plant, and safety support. Dennis wrote that he could prove that decentralizing decision making makes a company more efficient and profitable. But as CEO, the reason he did this was not for profitability, but because it was the right thing to do.

As Ray was giving away decisions to people in poor neighborhoods in Chicago, his younger brother was giving away decisions to front-line employees in electricity plants in Pakistan. Wall Street analysts were concerned that a headquarters staff of 100 in Washington, DC, could not manage a company of 40,000 employees on 4 continents effectively. National labor union leaders were confused about how to organize in power plants where union bosses were also plant managers. Stockholders were concerned that money was being invested to buy power plants in unstable locations such as Tbilisi, Georgia, former Soviet Union, which became the subject of the award-winning movie, *The Power Trip*, by Paul Devlin. In developing countries, stable electricity is one of the most effective means for common people to start businesses, improve the economy, and gain enough power to transform autocratic political structures that have existed for centuries.

Naming a School That Teaches Power-Distribution

In 2003, I was hired as the executive director of International Urban Associates (IUA), the Ray Bakke organization that continued the work of the Lausanne Committee on

World Evangelism. Combined, these organizations had held 250 city consultations in the world's largest cities over 25 years.. These consultations included government, business, church, education, and nonprofit leaders meeting for three to five days to discuss what was working well in their cities.

At the same time, Ray Bakke had recently assumed responsibility for a local education effort called the Northwest Graduate School of Ministry (NWGS), which was originally set up to provide Seattle-area pastors with doctoral and masters training. The school had almost collapsed and as Ray worked to rebuild NWGS, he realized it needed the full leadership resources of IUA to accomplish that task. The IUA board and the NWGS board voted to merge the two institutions and to create for advanced city leaders around the world a leadership network to experience peer learning and ongoing networking. This network would be called a *school* and would have accredited graduate programs. But the core identity was a *network*. We called it a network of advanced leaders in school's clothing.

However, we needed a new name. A friend of mine in Jakarta remarked, "Let me see. 'Northwest' as the name of a global school. Is it true that the center of the world's compass is Kansas?" So we went looking for a new name for the combined IUA and NWGS and hired naming consultants. I liked the name "Bridgehope University." Being the historical theologian, Ray liked ICTHUS (International Center for Theological Urban Studies). Others lobbied for International Urban University. Someone came up with the name Paradox University to describe the paradox of having an urban ministry school and a business school—traditional mortal enemies of each other—in the same university. The list grew to be quite large.

After months of surveys and work, the naming consultants gathered Ray and Dennis Bakke, me, and several of our board into a restaurant. They first said that names like "International" were great for missions agencies, but in the university branding world, that often signaled a degree mill. They told me "Bridgehope" sounded both English-centered and hokey. Names like ICTHUS and "Paradox" didn't get much comment except as examples of what not to do. They said that our mission was very different from what most people saw in a university or in urban ministry; we needed a fresh name that we could build meaning around.

The best names would be connected to a story that communicates the values of the organization we wanted to build.

Then they recommended that we name the school Bakke Graduate University, not for Ray or Dennis, but for the story of both brothers. It is a very unusual story for two brothers to pursue the exact same values of giving away power to others in two completely different arenas such as urban ministry and international business. By 2004, we had already constructed a mission statement and plan for the school so that it would include a theology-driven business school along with an urban-ministry theology school. The name and story of both brothers would show that these two fields, which rarely are taught together, could and should be taught together in the same family, as the lives of these two brothers demonstrated.

The story of the brothers reflected the common theology behind their life-missions. Both Ray and Dennis have persisted in promoting their view that decision-making power should be given away in spite of public criticism, stock market crashes following the Enron scandal, and even lawsuits. Why? Because it is the most important principle of urban ministry. It is the most important principle of a workplace that brings joy to its employees. It is consistent with what it means to be made in the image of God.

Image of God doesn't mean we look like Him.

> *Then God said, "Let us make man in our image, in our likeness, and let them rule over the fish of the sea and the birds of the air, over the livestock, over all the earth and over all the creatures that move along the ground." So God created man in his own image, in the image of God he created him; male and female he created them.*
>
> —Genesis 1:26–27

The primary Hebrew word for *image* in this verse is also used to describe the self-image often carved in stone by a king. This stone image was placed at the border of a conquered land to demonstrate to travelers they were entering a land that the king ruled. In ancient times, the ruling king didn't have access to cell phones, airplanes, or the Internet. The king often would appoint a governor over a distant land to make decisions on behalf of himself. It was impossible to consult the king on the majority of daily or even yearly decisions so, for most of the inhabitants of that land, the face of the governor was the face of the king. In that sense, the governor was the image of the king in flesh rather than instone. If the governor smiled at the people, then the king smiled at them. If the governor displayed anger toward the inhabitants, then the king was angry at them. It didn't mean the governor looked like the king. It meant the governor was given authority to make decisions on *behalf* of the king.

In the same way, when God made men and women in His image, He also gave them authority to make decisions on His behalf.

> *Now the LORD God had formed out of the ground all the beasts of the field and all the birds of the air. He brought them to the man to see what he would name them; and whatever the man called each living creature, that was its name. So the man gave names to all the livestock, the birds of the air and all the beasts of the field*
>
> — GENESIS 2;19–20

In this case, God was standing beside Adam. These animals were God's creation, not Adam's. I would assume that God, as the Creator of animals, might have an opinion about what would be a good or bad name for His creation. But the verse is worded very strongly that God did not interrupt, did not disagree, or did not overrule Adam's decision. Naming something that is not yours is a way to assume responsibility for it. God clearly was showing that Adam and Eve were to be the decision-makers on His behalf for all the created animals on the earth. When a porcupine saw Adam, he saw the image of God. When a tiger was given an order by Eve, it was by proxy, an order given by God Himself.

We don't know all it means to be made in God's image, but it does mean that we were created to work God's Creation and to make decisions on God's behalf. God intended us to work the Garden of Eden so He gave us opposable thumbs, an upright stance, and retracting muscles. Form follows function and our form is that of Garden-workers. Likewise, God also intended us to make decisions on His behalf and gave us the desire, responsibility, and ability to make decisions. We can conclude that we are also decision-making creatures.

As the firstborn of the Spirit—the new Adams and Eves—it is our core task on earth to demonstrate the good news of what it looks like to return to what God intended, and to tell people of the way God has provided for us to do that for eternity through Jesus Christ. Basically, we are the keepers of the vision of what it means to be made in the image of God. That is why it is so important that we lead urban ministries and businesses in ways that give away decision-making power.

Review

It is good urban ministry practice to give away decisions to people in the community where we minister. It is good spiritual formation practice to sacrifice our will in order to give away decision-making authority to those we serve. And, it is good theology to demonstrate to people God's original intention for us decision-making creatures made in God's image.

■ ■ ■ Personal Reflection

Where in your relationships, work, or service have you felt the most futility?

Did you find rest in a place of futility, or did you find yourself scrambling to overcome it or avoid it?

The goal of spiritual formation is to become less confident in yourself, more trusting of God, and more dependent on God and His work in our lives. Spiritual formation is not about us becoming more disciplined so we need God less. Spiritual disciplines are designed to help us habitually enter the place where we know that God is our Creator, we are His creatures, and we are in submission and dependence on Him. Spiritual disciplines practiced in a way that increases our confidence in our ability to pursue God through the strength of good habits and willpower actually takes us in the opposite direction. Where have you felt you have failed the most in trying to be a disciplined seeker of God?

How has that sense of failure helped you not to place your hope in your own efforts?

Spiritual formation often involves denying yourself that which you most desire in order to give to others what they need in their own journey. What about the principle discussed in this chapter—that the educated and experienced should give away decisions to the uneducated and inexperienced—makes sense or seems to be nonsense to you?

■ ■ ■ Bible Reflection

We live in a world that celebrates displays of strength and encourages self-expression and self-promotion as great virtues. Millions live vicariously through celebrities who go to outrageous lengths to out-express or out-promote each other. With repeated exposure in every aspect of our culture, these values quickly become part of our own culturally influenced, instinctive common sense.

Matthew 5:1–10 and 6;1–4 is about living in a state of dependence on God. These words celebrate as strength what others call "weakness."

(1) What in this passage is meant by "poor in spirit"?

"mourn"?

"meek"?

"hunger and thirst for righteousness"?

"merciful"?

"pure in heart"?

and "peacemaker"?

(2) What seems polar-opposite to our cultural common sense in these passages?

(3) How does the practice of giving away decision-making authority to others help you take on these characteristics?

Chapter Seven: INCARNATIONAL PRESENCE

Spiritual Formation Principle #7: God forms us when we commit to relationships among the least, the last, and the lost.

Theme: Incarnational presence is a commitment to God's call to a place, and the relationships, circumstances, and lifestyle that result from linking your present and future to the neighborhood.

Bible Reading:
Matthew 25:31–46

In 1990, I moved from Garrett Park in East Dallas to plant a church in the first-ring neighborhood immediately southwest of downtown Dallas. We had a small core of seven families but a doctrinal argument broke out early in the process so we lost two of these.

The neighborhood was in North Oak Cliff. When people in other parts of Dallas asked where we lived and we told them "Oak Cliff," they would respond by saying, "Oh! as thoughts of violent scenes on the 10 P.M. news went through their heads. We jokingly called their response the Oak Cliff "Oh!"

Actually, the neighborhood I was moving from was even worse for me so, Oak Cliff was an upgrade to a place that had sidewalks and beautiful rows of old single-family houses; quite a contrast to the abandoned lots and burned-out apartment complexes of Garrett Park.

Oak Cliff was also different in how I felt about the neighborhood. I didn't feel so intimidated and guarded. I felt secure and curious from the first day. Partly it was because I was a pastor, not just an urban worker creating a beachhead for others to follow. The local church has a unique position and responsibility to the area where it is located. I felt this was my parish so I needed to know every nook and cranny. In part, I think this was because the people in my core group had a contagious love for this place and they were introducing me to all of their friends.

Mostly, it was because God was giving me a taste of His love for this place. Other urban workers have described this phenomenon. It makes little sense, but God seems to bless our commitment to a place with a supernatural love for a location—its people, the way it looks, its smells—everything.

I walked most of the neighborhood, taking in the details. Then I got on my motorcycle and slowly rode the streets just outside the immediate blocks closest to where the church was meeting. I was working some Saturdays to facilitate collaboration meetings at a nonprofit event center sponsored by a large foundation. It had off-duty police officers always present, sitting and watching by security cameras. Several knew my new neighborhood well. I sat for hours, pumping them with questions about where the crime centers were, who the leaders they worked with were, and what were the secrets that only the police knew. It is amazing how many secrets a neighborhood holds in its history, political leaders, parks, and businesses.

My next-door neighbor was a Native American leader who had lived there for 40 years. He told stories of the gigantic 1957 tornado that took out three houses immediately south of his own, hit his concrete house directly but left it standing, and left my backyard garage in a precarious slant to this day. I found the grave where Clyde Barrow (a.k.a. Bonnie and Clyde) was buried in the Western Heights Cemetery about one-half mile north of my house. I dug through weeds to find the nearby historical marker of the first settlement in Dallas, called La Reunion, a failed socialist utopian community formed in 1855. I explored the location of the notable convenience store eight blocks away. I found the location near my house where, in 1963, Lee Harvey Oswald had shot police officer J. D. Tippit. The neighborhood history, people, and terrain captured me.

I determined to sample every restaurant within a one-mile radius. I attended the hearings that preceded the historic dismantling of the largest housing projects in Texas, about two miles north of my house. I made appointments to meet nearby school principals and city officials. I used to sit with a map while eating breakfast, memorizing street names and looking for places I hadn't yet seen.

Each afternoon, I'd take walks and end up on a neighbor's porch, hearing his or her stories. Later, my own front porch became a regular gathering place, even if I wasn't home. As the church grew, visitors would tell me where they lived. Most were surprised that I knew where their street was. In sermons, I talked about the historic places I found or conversations I had with city officials, revealing some interesting fact about our neighborhood. Visitors who were longtime residents would come up to tell me other little known facts or express their surprise that a newbie like me would know facts that they had not heard of before.

Ray Bakke, too, talks about his experience of reading the city of Chicago and unearthing the treasures he found in his neighborhood. As you watch his energy as he talks about Chicago, you realize quickly that this is not an academic accounting of an urban ministry strategy.

Looking back, I can't say that all this energy to discover so much about this place in such a short time was a conscious urban-ministry strategy. I was almost obsessed! I couldn't seem to get enough information about my neighborhood. Even now, when I drive back into the neighborhood, I get a feeling like this is the most beautiful neighborhood in the world. Memories from this time seem more visually vivid than at other times in my life. I love to drive through the neighborhood and point out sights and tell stories to my children who were born after I left North Oak Cliff.

There is a "theology of place." God calls us to a place to be present; totally immersed as His agent of transforming presence. We are called to commit to a location for time periods and serve whatever needs arise there. Many people describe a theology of place as a duty—something you commit to in order to be an effective minister. For me, it was almost a romance. As I describe this to others, they laugh and say that, in actuality, their experience was similar—even in some fairly ugly, dysfunctional neighborhoods. What is odd is that in these places we experienced great frustration, sadness, and painful events in our lives and in the lives of people we loved. But somehow God often provides a peace and joy that surpasses understanding, that comes in a package deal with His call to a place.

I even feel a pang of sadness as I drive through and wonder how life would be different if I had stayed. But several years after I had moved into North Oak Cliff, God called me to leave and He knew I needed help to secure this decision. I had been offered a new ministry in a different city and had finally made the decision to move. However, I had not yet told anyone, not even my new employers. After one Sunday sermon, our bookkeeper Mary Ann came up and asked for a chance to talk to me privately. Mary Ann was quiet and often suspicious of what she thought was sensationalism by charismatic Christians who attended that church. She looked very nervous. She said she had had a dream the night before and that God told her that I was planning to leave. More specifically, God had told her that I was worried and needed to be encouraged. She said God told her that it was OK. I was supposed to leave. Mary Anne said she was sorry if this didn't make any sense to me and she was embarrassed but felt she had to tell me about the dream. God knew I needed something supernatural to release me from the place to which He had supernaturally bonded me.

The Mantle

God often calls us to commit to a place. God often accompanies that call with an unusual curiosity—if not supernatural love—for that place. Even beyond that, God sometimes accompanies this call and love with a mantle of influence that goes beyond common sense.

The word *mantle* is an older English word for *cloak*. In 2 Kings 2, the story is told of Elijah walking with his successor Elisha.

> As they were walking along and talking together, suddenly a chari-
> ot of fire and horses of fire appeared and separated the two of them,
> and Elijah went up to heaven in a whirlwind. Elisha saw this and

cried out, "My father! My father! The chariots and horsemen of Israel!" And Elisha saw him no more. Then he took hold of his own clothes and tore them apart. He picked up the cloak that had fallen from Elijah and went back and stood on the bank of the Jordan. Then he took the cloak that had fallen from him and struck the water with it. "Where now is the Lord, the God of Elijah?" he asked. When he struck the water, it divided to the right and to the left, and he crossed over. The company of the prophets from Jericho, who were watching, said, "The spirit of Elijah is resting on Elisha." And they went to meet him and bowed to the ground before him."

—2 Kings 2:11–15

It seems as if God gives people a special cloak of influence that is connected to a place and time, in a similar fashion to how God used Elijah's cloak to demonstrate the transfer of influence and authority to Elishah.

Recently I visited a student of Bakke Graduate University, a blond, blue-eyed US American who lives in Central America's most violent city, Guatemala City. Much of the violence is a result of ruthless warfare between the two most dangerous and largest gangs in the world, the 18th Street gang and the Mara Salvatrucha (MS13). Through an unusual series of coincidences, that is "God incidents", he was asked by the Guatemalan prison authorities to develop a team of chaplains to minister to members of these gangs in prison. Even more supernatural, he and his chaplains gained the approval of the gang leaders to come into their prison areas.

He invited me to join him and his chaplains on a recent visit. We were ushered to an area of the prison far removed from the general population. The guards looked at us like we were fools as they unlocked several layers of doors, let us go ahead, as they remained out of gang members' sight. In an instant, I was locked in a small general area with 120 gang members, most of whom had tattoos all over their bodies, including their foreheads, eyelids, and cheeks. Several people have asked me since that time if I felt frightened. The answer is of course yes, but only for a short time.

First, I was under the natural mantle of the gang leaders. They had given the order to protect the chaplains and their guests. In that prison, I was probably safer than I am sitting behind locked doors in my own house in the US. These gangs have a severe loyalty and are disciplined by a strict code that makes the mantle of their leaders a powerful force. But more importantly, I was in the cell with my friend and he had a supernatural mantle.

Before my chaplain friend's arrival, these prisoners never left their 10-by-15 foot cells shared by six (up to 12 in some cases). In less than nine months, my friend's and his chaplains' visits to the cells had calmed down the turmoil in the cells so that, for the first time since this unit had been established, the gang members were allowed out of their individual cells to roam in the general area, which was about 20-by-100 feet. In this prison, there was no outside exercise area or cafeteria. Most prisoners had terms of more than 15 years. Some had terms of more than 140 years. Because of the decisions they had made at 14 or 15 years old, they would live much of their lives never leaving this small area. It was a sign of supernatural influence and blessing to all involved that the chaplains would be the vehicle to add even 2,000 more feet of freedom.

As we arrived, a group of gang members was working on a table, making silk screen shirts ordered by a computer company in Virginia. One of the members gave me two intricately braided pins, with my school's logo—a sales sample in case we wanted to give them more orders. Some of the money they have gained from previous sales had been donated to a local orphanage.

Certainly, many of the gang members hid in their cells as we arrived. But others came up with excitement and warmth—big grins behind evil-looking tattoos. With 120 gang members living their lives together in cramped spaces, there remained a code of hardness. The regular visit by the chaplains was one of the few times it made sense for them to smile. They told their stories. A few shared small dreams. I believe what God had done through my friend in such a short time was unprecedented in any prison gang ministry in any prison, most certainly in a Central American prison with these particular gangs.

This is what Ray Bakke discusses as "common grace." Because of my friend's presence, the gang members had been blessed with substantialy more room in their imprisonment, even if they had no interest whatsoever in hearing about Jesus. The guards were less on edge. Guatemalan political figures were less worried about another riot and massacre from an in-prison war between gangs. Some orphans received additional clothing, food, and care.

A few of the gang members also experienced *saving grace*. They learned that God loves them so much that He became a man in the form of Jesus Christ. He lived a perfect life, then died on the Cross in substitution for all of us. He was resurrected and will come back some day and return the world to a place without sin and pain. Each person has a choice to accept the gift and join God for eternity. Or they can reject the gift and live out eternity separated from God, which is torment for humans who were created to be in connection with God.

Both of these graces come from God. Both are activated by the presence of my friend in this prison.

Incarnational Ministry

The call to a place that is followed by a commitment, even a love and perhaps a supernatural mantle is *incarnational* ministry. The word usually applies to God the Spirit taking on the flesh of humankind as Jesus Christ did. When applied to urban ministry, it means that a "person becomes one of us." It means moving into a neighborhood and taking on the same circumstances of joy and pain that everyone else is experiencing. It means connecting to the hopes and destinies of the people of the neighborhood. It is living life *among* and *with* those who we are ministering among and with.

For years, it was assumed that incarnational ministry and a theology of place always meant packing up and living in a poor neighborhood. However, in recent years, the meaning has been expanded to include those whose hearts are in a place, but whose call is to live elsewhere.

Advocates

Several years ago in Dallas, I was in a backroom conversation that John Perkins was leading. John Perkins is one of the fathers and leaders of modern urban ministry, working tirelessly for almost 50 years to teach and demonstrate the life of Jesus Christ among the poor, disenfranchised, and powerless. Early in his ministry, he was challenged by how to explain what he did to supporters and volunteers who were joining the ministry from the outside. He boiled down his philosophy to the three R's of Development:

Reconciliation—between people groups, cultures, and socioeconomic groups

Relocation—moving into the urban centers to live and minister among the poor

Redistribution—transferring money, power, and knowledge from those who have it to those who don't.

For those who grew up in the first generation of urban ministry of the 1970s and 1980s, all three of these were sacred. If you weren't doing all three, then you were only a pretender in urban ministry. It was a powerful but unwritten rule not to listen to anyone who had not paid their dues by living in a bad neighborhood. Nobody could teach us unless they could demonstrate they had experienced pain, scars, and the humiliation of moving headlong into reconciliation, and the ostracizing that comes from speaking strongly for redistribution.

Yet in Dallas, at this late night meeting, John raised the question, "Do you think that maybe God has genuinely called some people to urban ministry, but has not called them to relocate?" I immediately felt my head burn as I thought. *We all had paid those dues. Most of the lessons we learned were on the streets. There was no way you could learn those lessons or be trusted if you had not relocated. No one should be let in who had not paid the dues that we had paid.*

I stayed quiet and watched. Many in the room had paid dues far greater than I had. Some had grown up in a bad neighborhood, gained the means to leave, then chose to return. Their sacrifice was far greater than mine. I also realized their anger was far greater than mine too. It made a lot of sense to me to not say a word.

It was a passionate discussion. John's point was that urban ministry was quickly moving to a point where advocacy was becoming more important than before. After the Welfare Reform legislation of 1996 in the US, the money for social programs was increasingly coming from local and even business sources rather than Washington, D.C.-based government sources. It was his experience that God could have a profound impact on the hearts of people in places of power, privilege, and money to steward these things for people who are powerless, disenfranchised, and poor. Yet, he observed that they could do more good for the neighborhood by staying where they were. There was a new role that God was creating that had always been present, but was increasing suddenly in almost every city that he visited. What was more surprising is that the hearts of these people in this advocacy role demonstrated a humility he had not seen before. God was doing something that no one could explain apart from supernatural means.

The discussion was interrupted, but the buzz continued for the rest of the conference. A second stage of urban ministry was rising, but it was firmly connected to and dependent on the first-stage foundation. The three R's were more important than ever, but their definitions included some new components. God was preparing an increased role for the outside champion, who submitted to the agenda of the neighborhood. The role of business was moving from adversary to advocate. There was a place for the voice of the outsider.

Proverbs 31:8–9 reads, *"Speak up for those who cannot speak for themselves, for the rights of all who are destitute. Speak up and judge fairly; defend the rights of the poor and needy."*

Body Guards

When I was president of Leadership Network, I had the privilege to serve under a board that was led by Chairperson Jack Willome. Jack had served as the president of Rayco, one of the largest home-building companies in Texas, based in San Antonio. As chairperson of Leadership Network, a sister organization called The Gathering, and another ministry at Laity Lodge, Jack oversaw organizations that held several large national events each year. These events invited the best speakers and Bible teachers in North America.

Yet, in the late 1990s, Jack was drawn to visit an inner-city ministry called Victory Outreach, led by Alfredo "Freddie" Garcia. As Freddie taught the Book of Romans to recovering drug addicts, Jack told me that the Bible teaching he heard there from a gritty, uneducated, but intensely real Bible teacher, was the best he had ever heard. Jack became a regular fixture at the Garcia house, which had a perpetually active kitchen and a stream of people coming in and out, sleeping on the floors and in the hallways, and crowding into small rooms to listen to Freddie's Bible teaching.

Dressed in pressed shirts and shined shoes, Jack looked like a visitor from Mars on the North San Eduardo Street. Freddie told Jack that he would protect him in his neighborhood. Jack realized that, without this protection, he would not survive.

Victory Outreach was started in 1972 to help people on the streets to overcome drug addictions. For almost 30 years, it was located in a two-bedroom, blue house that had been converted into vastly overcrowded men's and women's dormitories with various back rooms, side rooms, and outbuildings added throughout the years. However, Freddie had always dreamed of buying a nearby abandoned lot. He dreamed of building better facilities on the lot so he could take in more men and women coming off the streets.

As Jack kept hanging out for weeks, then months, then years, Freddie began to increasingly trust this strange visitor from another world in San Antonio. When Jack asked about Freddie's dream, Freddie told him that he had tried to buy the land several times, but the buyer would not sell and he didn't have enough money to make a serious offer. Finally Freddie gained enough trust of Jack to ask him to help.

After a few weeks of research, Jack discovered that Freddie had been depositing a few dollars each week into a noninterest-bearing account in a local bank. Most of the money had come from small donations from recovering addicts, who wanted to express their gratitude for Victory Outreach's dramatic invention in their lives that had been careening toward disaster. Over the years, the deposits had added up to almost $1 million. No one in the bank had taken the time to explain to Freddie how this money could be invested so, while the amount was large, it was not nearly as large as it could have been if it had been placed in an interest-bearing account.

Jack knew many of the directors and officers of the bank and was angry at how the bank had abused Freddie's lack of knowledge to benefit their financial position. He was also amazed that someone as street-wise as Freddie could be conned out of so much money. As he talked to Freddie about this, Freddie replied, "When you come into my neighborhood, you wouldn't survive without my protection. But the bank is your neighborhood, not mine. As I have protected you here, I needed someone like you to protect me there."

A few years later, Jack used his relationships and skills to help Freddie purchase the land with both the money he saved and money "donated" by the bank that equaled much of what was lost in the years of being in a noninterest-bearing account. Today Victory Outreach is serving more people than ever in clean, efficient, and much larger facilities on the new property Jack helped Freddie to buy.

Jack had not relocated his family to the 'hood, but he had relocated his heart there. Some urban leaders criticized Jack for continuing to live in a nice house in a nice suburb. He had submitted himself to Freddie and other leaders in the neighborhood in ways that drew criticism from leaders in the suburbs. Yet, Jack's call was to bless with his presence as a regular visitor, and to advocate with his position; a new kind of urban minister.

■ ■ ■ Personal Reflection

Describe what a *theology of place* means to you. How have you experienced it?

Are you called to incarnational ministry somewhere? Does your call also include a call to relocate to that place?

■ ■ ■ Bible Reflection

Ephesians 2:8–9 reads: *"For it is by grace you have been saved, through faith—and this not from yourselves, it is the gift of God—not by works, so that no one can boast."*

Read Matthew 25:31–46. We know from Ephesians 2 and many other places in Scripture that our eternal salvation does not come from our acts of service to the hungry, thirsty, stranger, naked, and prisoner. Yet, there is something about having a motivation to serve these that flows from our salvation and is a sign of God's saving work in us. How do you see this passage describing the actions of a genuine follower of Christ?

How do you think Jesus is so closely identified with those in need?

Chapter Eight: WHOLE GOSPEL

Spiritual Formation Principle #8: We are formed by proclaiming a gospel and living a life that reconciles us with God, ourselves, each other, and our world.

Theme: Urban ministry in hostile contexts such as Africa requires presence, shrewdness, and holistic ministry.

Bible Reading:
Genesis 3:1–13, 16–19
Matthew 10:16
Romans 8:12–24*a*

Islam was founded in the late sixth and early seventh century by Muhammad. By the mid-eighth century it had expanded to include a large geographic area called a *caliphate*, ruled by religious leaders. Islam believes that Muhammad did not found a new religion, but was the last and greatest prophet in the succession of prophets that included Abraham, Moses, Jesus, and others. Islam believes that the message of prophets, such as Abraham, Moses, and Jesus, was distorted by the Jews and others and Muhammad was sent to provide a correction. Many Muslims today see their religion as an important correction to Judaism and Christianity, but see the greatest threat to their faithfulness coming from secular philosophies and lifestyles, such as materialism, hedonism, and other influences brought into their lives by globalism and technology. Even the largest Muslim country in the world, Indonesia, is attempting to practice a form of Islam called "Civil Islam" that shares some of the same practical goals that Christians call the "Cultural Mandate" of Genesis 1:28.

However, the radical element of fundamentalist Islam is very different. Radical Islam today believes that the Caliphate of former centuries should be restored into a united political kingdom under Islamic Law, *sharia*, that includes detailed rules about dress, behavior, diets, banking, warfare, and almost every area of life.

The eighth-century Caliphate included all of the Middle East, as far east as territory in Afghanistan and Pakistan today. It enveloped the southern border of the Mediterranean Sea, across North Africa, and even wrapped north to include Spain. In the area targeted for the restoration of a modern-day Caliphate, some would also include later areas of influence, such as modern-day Somalia, Sudan, parts of Ethiopia, and a southern buffer zone across much of subSaharan Africa. South of this huge band across Africa, stretching through northern Nigeria all the way to Senegal on the west coast, is an area with a very fast-growing Christian influence today. It is not surprising then that the conflict areas of these two faiths in our generation are often found in the major cities of this region in Africa.

As delineated by Paul Berman in "The Philosopher of Islamic Terror," an article in the *New York Times Magazine*, a 20th-century Islamic philosopher named Sayyid Qutb wrote a book that is widely held as the classic manifesto of the terrorist wing of Islamic fundamentalism. A basic theme of Qutb's writings is that Jesus's disciples were persecuted by the Jews and that this drove them to the Greek world where Jesus's words were horribly distorted by the dualistic thinking of the Greeks. As a result, Qutb believes that Christians can say one thing about what they believe in their Spirit, but then act in totally contradictory ways in the actions of their bodies. He posits this dualistic thinking from the West has influenced the secular governments of countries such as Saudi Arabia and others. For Islam to survive, Qutb wrote, the Western influence must be removed from the area where the Caliphate must be restored. These secular governments in the region must be replaced with a united government, all under Islamic law. At this point, Iran is the only beachhead for this new Caliphate.

Islam is a religion where an individual's personal faithfulness is dependent on his surroundings. Islamic laws remove temptations. Women cover themselves from head to foot to remove men's temptation to lust and adultery. Alcohol is banned. There are strict requirements to pray at established times during the day, enforced by police and peers. In Islam, these strict rules for the actions of the body are absolutely necessary for the formation of the spirit.

In stark contrast, the Christian individual's personal faith is dependent on the indwelling of the Holy Spirit. No matter what is happening in the Christian's surrounding culture, there is power within to live a life of personal holiness. Because of the indwelling of the Holy Spirit and the forgiveness of sin, the actions of the body are very important but are not absolutely necessary for the formation of the spirit.

Those of us who live in the United States certainly wish that our culture wasn't in such a rapid moral decline. A major obstacle to my spiritual formation is cultural influence. I realize that my spiritual health would be much greater if the actions of my body were more disciplined and in sync with what I believe. There are times that I envy those who are "forced" to have a daily routine of prayer. However, we don't view the future of Christianity, or even the faithfulness of our spiritual walk, as absolutely connected to the vast moral decline of our culture. In places such as China, where the government tried to create a strong secular culture that warred against Christianity from the mid 1950s to the late 1970s,, Christianity flourished during that time. Christianity is much more flexible and adaptable because its power comes from God within, not from culture without.

The radical Islamic fundamentalists believe that unless they stop secular influences from the West and destroy secular governments in the region where the Caliphate should be restored, Islam will die. Terrorism is an extreme act because what they believe in is under extreme attack.

Islam has always emphasized expansion through a show of strength. When former Christian areas were conquered, often they would tear down the cathedrals and churches and rebuild a mosque on the ruins. Most were designed to be larger than the buildings they replaced. The Dome of the Rock sits over the site formerly occupied by the Jewish temple. The Blue Mosque in Istanbul (Sultan Ahmed Mosque) was built with the express purpose of showing architectural superiority over the adjacent Hagia Sophia, built almost 1,100 years earlier as a Christian church. For Islam, the show of strength through buildings and political power is an important part of their expansion strategy.

Addis Ababa, Ethiopia, is one place where Islam meets Christianity and the starkly contrasting styles of evangelism and urban ministry are clearly demonstrated. Judaism was a major force in Ethiopia from the time of King Solomon. Christianity traces its roots back to the encounter between Phillip and the Ethiopian eunuch in Acts 8. Having converted to Christianity during the fourth century A.D., it is the second-oldest country after Armenia to become an official Christian nation.

Several large foundations in the Middle East are active in Addis Ababa, buying land and building huge mosques throughout the city. Throughout the day, gigantic loudspeakers on the mosques blare out calls and prayers declaring an "air war" superiority over the Christians who live under the torturous sounds. To fill these new mosques, people are often paid to attend in order to demonstrate to the neighborhoods the dominance of Islam over this former Christian territory. It is intimidating to be a Christian in this area where Islam is conducting a "shock and awe" show of force to expand its borders.

While Christianity has also expanded through a show of force at times, Jesus instructed us in Matthew 28 to expand by teaching people to obey all that He taught. Certainly in Matthew 5, Jesus did not teach dominance by a show of force. His life was an example of submission to the will of His Father, even to the point of what appeared in human eyes to be a political and physical defeat on the Cross.

In the center of Addis Ababa is a ministry led by Bakke Graduate University Regent Jember Teferra. Her great-uncle was the last emperor of Ethiopia who traces his lineage back to the Menelik I, the purported son of King Solomon and the Queen of Sheba. Her husband was the mayor of Addis Ababa in the early 1970s. After a bloody military Marxist revolution in 1974, Jember was arrested as a political prisoner and spent five years in jail.

Even in jail, Jember created a health ministry to both prisoners and guards. Since that time, she has created a large housing, health, and education ministry for the poor of Addis Ababa, earning the prestigious MaAFRIKA award in 2001 for her outstanding humanitarian efforts. Surrounded by impressive Islamic monoliths, under the sound of blaring Islamic prayer speakers, and without the massive financial resources that are being used to pay people to attend impressive Islamic shows of force, Jember is quietly conducting a large urban ministry of presence, love, and care.

In a way, it is a contest between strength and humility, force and incarnation. Her work is growing much faster without paid participants than the Islamic ministries are growing with the influx of resources. Many of those who attend the mosques to meet their financial needs return to Jember's ministry to have their heart-needs met.

Urban Ministry in a Hostile Context

I've discussed with Jember how she is able to be so effective in the face of so much intimidation and I have attempted to synthesize these conversations into a few key principles:

(1) **Presence:** Jember's ministers are present in the neighborhood in mass numbers. There are thousands of people in life-on-life relationships where she serves. Western missions tend to want to do something "big and strategic"—take a swing for the home-run fence. Her approach is to be present and faithful. People *react* to receiving resources, but people *commit* when relationships accompany those resources.

(2) **Shrewdness:** Matthew 10:16 states: *"I am sending you out like sheep among wolves. Therefore be as shrewd as snakes and as innocent as doves."* In Jember's context, the wolves are very obvious and scream their taunts on loudspeakers many times a day. Additionally, city officials are continually coming up with schemes to move her housing developments, under the guise of "capital improvements," or trying to manipulate the laws to target her directly. As a result, Jember has to minister:

(a) Politically—"Who is in power and how do I build relationships with them and influence them to make decisions in my favor?"

(b) Publically—"How do I develop enough publicity with outside interests so local officials know that they will have intense outside pressure if they shut me down?"

(c) Prayerfully—"How do I continually evoke the supernatural power of God in this situation, where in the natural realm I have so many disadvantages?"

(3) Holistic: The name of Jember's ministry is the Integrated Holistic Approach Urban Development Project (IHA-UDP). In her African setting, telling people how to accept Jesus Christ without first helping them overcome their hunger, homelessness, or health problems feels like the same category as trying to sell a latte machine to someone who lives in a cardboard box without electricity. There is no context for such people to understand you and what you are offering them. In her ministry, the sharing of the good news about Christ's death occurs as people are also receiving the good news that their infant will have the nutrition and medicines to live beyond six months old. When people see their survival needs met, there is the trust and relationship to talk about their eternal needs. Christian urban leaders in Africa, such as Jember, don't have the same legacy of dualistic ministry inherited in the United States, so holistic ministry seems to be the natural way to do it.

Bad News

In Genesis 3, there seems to be evidence of four types of breaks that occurred as a result of Eve and Adam eating the apple (or pomegranate) off the Tree of the Knowledge of Good and Evil. These four breaks include:

(1) Between us and God. In Genesis 3:8, God is walking in the Garden in the cool of the day. The phrasing creates the assumption that this was a normal

occurrence; perhaps a daily visit and walk between the Creator and Adam and Eve to discuss the events of the day. Normally, Adam and Eve perhaps would run to greet God, excitedly talking about a new thing they had learned about His creation. This time they hid. They had disobeyed. They had rebelled. No longer was theirs a seamless fellowship between God and the governors of His creation. His will was no longer their will. They had created a second and third will on the earth in addition to God's. As a result, their children would each be born with individual wills that from birth would immediately take a different path than God's will. Humans were created to be in relationship with God. To lose that relationship has created a profound vacuum as we have lost the very core of our identity.

(2) Between us and ourselves. In Genesis 3:10, when God calls out looking for Adam and Eve, Adam responds that he hid because he was afraid of God; because he was naked. Before the fall, Adam was comfortable in his own skin. He didn't feel fear of God or anything else. He wasn't afraid of being naked. Some people observe that even after humans were kicked out of the Garden of Eden, they lived much longer lives than today—up to 969 years in the case of Methuselah (5:25). The further the generations got from the Garden, the shorter their lifespan. It is assumed that we were originally created to live much longer than we do now. If we had remained in the garden, there would be no genetic disease, no birth defects, no addictions, and no unhealthy eating. Perhaps humans were also stronger, and more emotionally expressive. Today our bodies have all sorts of illnesses; we rarely understand or have control over our emotions; we disconnect easily from the reality around us; we don't have discipline over our own actions; and we feel deep shame, fear, insecurities, and confusion. We are mere shadows of what Adam and Eve were and God intended us to be.

(3) Between us and each other. Immediately after eating the forbidden fruit, Adam and Eve sew fig leaves to cover up. They are no longer connected so closely as "one flesh" and now they feel the need to cover up their differences. In Genesis 3:12, Adam is blaming Eve for the situation—distancing himself from a decision they both made (Genesis 3:6 says "Adam was with her.") In chapter 4 we read

about one of the first siblings' killing; one out of jealousy. Humans were created to live in deep relationship with each other. We all seek for a profound connection with our spouse, children, friends, parents, and siblings, that we never find. We've lost much of our core purpose and sustaining energy in our lives.

(4) Between us and our world. Before the fall, Adam and Eve ate fruit (and probably vegetables) and didn't need leather clothes or shoes, so the animals had no reason to fear them. They had greater abilities to communicate with the animals we were created to rule over. I can almost see Adam and Eve laughing, working side by side with each other and animals. If they wanted something heavy moved, the elephant probably could have helped. If they wanted the ground broken up a bit, we might imagine that the moles might have prepared the ground,. If the ripest fruit in a tree was above their reach, the giraffe might have plucked it for his loving caretakers. That was the life we were designed to live. Genesis 2:15 identifies humans as garden-working creatures. But the fall placed us as garden creatures in the ghetto, far removed from the world for which we were designed.

God tells Adam that now the ground will grow weeds which will make his work futile (Genesis 3:17–18). The weeds now form a barrier that disconnect him from his created purpose. Like an eagle on a chain, a tiger in a parking lot, or a dolphin in a bathtub, Adam is separated from his Garden. All that he desires to do results in some degree of futility.

Solomon, arguably the wisest person in history and certainly a person who had more of anything he wanted than any of us will ever attain, starts his book by exclaiming:

"Meaningless! Meaningless!" says the Teacher. "Utterly meaningless! Everything is meaningless. What does man gain from all his labor at which he toils under the sun?" (Ecclesiastes 1:2–3). Solomon, one of the richest, most powerful, and God-blessed persons in the history of the world, concluded life is futile in between the Garden and the New Jerusalem.

We all strive for an antidote to futility in the next promotion, next new car, or next attempt to manipulate our spouse or kids to do what we want. Perhaps it is time to realize none of us will ever create a rocket to overcome the gravitational pull of futility in our lives. As a result of the breaks between us and our world, we now are destroying our environment; we have massive inequalities between the food we produce and those who need it; we have natural disasters that kill us; we are plagued with diseases; and we never reach a place where we are satisfied to the depth of our soul, no matter how hard we work or how much success we attain.

Good News

The four breaks are the bad news of the fall and the resulting curse of Genesis 3. So if this is the bad news, wouldn't it make sense that the good news that Jesus came to tell us is that God has provided a way for all four of these breaks to be restored—in full in the future but, in part, in our world right now? God's Word tells us,

> I consider that our present sufferings are not worth comparing with the glory that will be revealed in us. The creation waits in eager expectation for the sons of God to be revealed. For the creation was subjected to frustration, not by its own choice, but by the will of the one who subjected it, in hope that the creation itself will be liberated from its bondage to decay and brought into the glorious freedom of the children of God. We know that the whole creation has been groaning as in the pains of childbirth right up to the present time. Not only so, but we ourselves, who have the firstfruits of the Spirit, groan inwardly as we wait eagerly for our adoption as sons, the redemption of our bodies. For in this hope we were saved.
>
> —ROMANS 8:18–24A

The good news is that, because of Jesus's death and resurrection, there are now four restorations that make up the full gospel:

(1) Between us and God

(2) Between us and ourselves

(3) Between us and each other

(4) Between us and our world

We can experience these four restorations, in part now and in full when Jesus returns in Revelation 19 with a sword in His mouth, and then lowers the New Jerusalem to earth in Revelation 21.

For much of history, there have been alternating times when this full gospel was presented and when one or various parts of it were left out. In the 1800s, Christians, who were sometimes labeled evangelical, spoke of and demonstrated all four aspects of this gospel. Organizations that did evangelism and social action together emerged, including The City Mission Movement (1826), The Salvation Army (1878), and a host of other local and international movements.

At the same time, however, a group of theologians was applying modernistic, Enlightenment thought to Christianity in a movement called "Liberal Christianity." It was a very complex movement with many veins. Some were concluding, among other thoughts, that the Bible was made up of many myths, and that the concept of God may be an invention of humans. If there is strong doubt that God actually exists as a Person outside of creation, then the first of the four restorations of the gospel listed above doesn't make sense. As a result, religious liberals continued to call themselves Christians, but emphasized restorations number two through four as the actual gospel. This is sometimes called "The Social Gospel."

A group called *fundamentalists* formed in reaction to this and emphasized that restoration number one is the actual gospel. The gospel was then bifurcated, with restorations number two through four being claimed by the social gospel side and restoration number one being claimed by the fundamentalist side. Over time, the label "evangelical" in the United States became synonymous in the US media with the "fundamentalist" camp.

For almost a century, the four restorations of the gospel was bifurcated between two opposing groups in the US and much of the Western-influenced church.

Arguably, as the 20th century ended, the power, size, and influence of liberal Christendom has greatly waned in the US. Religious liberalism is still taught in many seminaries and while numbers are greatly diminished, there are still mainline denominations that hold to the tenets of religious liberalism. As Christianity has exploded in the southern hemisphere and Asia, it rarely demonstrated the tenets of liberal Christianity, further decreasing the percentage of world Christians who support the tenets of liberal Christianity.

So in most cases, the "war" that bifurcated the four restorations of the gospel is over. As we begin the 21st century, the church is faced with the opportunity to re-connect the bifurcated gospel into a holistic gospel. For those coming from the number one camp, at first it appears that by adding numbers two, three, and four, it is a sell-out to liberalism. In fact, it is restoring the original evangelical message. For most Christian leaders in the areas where Christianity is growing the fastest, the message of four restorations is already what they are presenting as healthy Christianity. Most never went through the wars of gospel "bifurcation." Those that are aware of it realize that you cannot bifurcate these four restorations of the gospel when you work in cultures where Christianity is not the majority worldview. Bridges have to be built to people with demonstration of the gospel before they have the context and relationship to understand the message of the gospel.

Most people with a high view of Scriptures still emphasize the unique aspect of restoration; the restoration between God and man is the ultimate message of the gospel, that lasts for eternity and is the reason and power for restoration between us and ourselves; between us and each other; and between us and our world. However, the latter restorations are how we demonstrate the results of the restoration between God and humankind to people who don't have the context or relationship to even begin to understand what we are talking about in discussing our restoration to God. This is what is often called the *holistic gospel*—a gospel of both word and deed; good news and good deeds.

■ ■ ■ Personal Reflection

Even though you may not face the same overt pressures against your Christianity as what was described in Africa, what type of pressures do you face?

In what ways are presence, shrewdness, and a holistic gospel part of how you respond to these pressures?

How do you see love as more effective than strength in how you've been influenced personally?

How would you restate the idea of the four breaks in Genesis 3 being the four reconciliations of the whole gospel?

What about this do you agree with, disagree with, or is just a new way to express what you were thinking already?

■ ■ ■ Bible Reflection

Read Genesis 3:1–13, 16–19.

The temptation story is not about being hungry. With what were Eve and Adam actually tempted?

In what ways were Adam and Eve personally cursed, and in what ways was their environment cursed?

Read Matthew 10:16.

Why would Jesus tell His disciples to be shrewd as well as innocent?

What are some examples of shrewd, yet innocent behaviors?

Read Romans 8:12–24*a*.
What does it mean personally to be a son or daughter of God?

What is different in your life as a result?

What does it mean publicly to be a son or daughter of God?

What is different about your call in life as a result?

Chapter Nine: HAND, HEART, AND HEAD FORMATION

Spiritual Formation Principle #9: Spiritual formation activities can be confusing and complicated unless we pursue them in ways that are consistent with how God has wired us, and with a focus on this one true goal of all spiritual formation activities.

Theme: The goal of spiritual formation is to increase our trust and dependence on God as the deepest motives of our hearts.

Bible Reading
James 1–2

Spiritual Formation that Works

We all want to grow spiritually, but for most of us the journey is confusing. We know that God causes us to grow, yet our spiritual growth is not something we can control, plan, or totally understand. There are things that we do that either contribute to, or detract from, what God is doing in our lives. The term that is often used to describe **our** contribution is *spiritual formation*.

A few decades ago, this term was mostly a Catholic term. Originally it had strong connection with the use of a spiritual director, who provided a sort of weekly counseling appointment to people who were serious about spiritual growth. In contrast, evangelicals often use the word *discipleship* to communicate our effort to cooperate with God as *He* forms us spiritually. No matter what term we use, the topic is something that we all spend a great deal of time pursuing, but most of us wonder why so much effort often results in so little growth.

There are many sermons and Christian conferences on the topic of spiritual growth. When the topic of spiritual formation or discipleship comes up, there is almost 100 percent agreement that this involves certain activities. Most spiritual formation or discipleship sermons advocate three important activities:

(1) Prayer—private and corporate, often in a "quiet time" each morning

(2) Bible study—private, family, and church-wide

(3) Regular attendance—church or mass, that includes "means of grace," such as corporate worship, communion, the preaching of the word, and fellowship

A topic that is broader and often harder to define, but that is discussed and implied as a non-negotiable part of the first three activities is:

(4) Obedience—readiness to confess sin, repent of wrong, and make a sincere effort to do what is right.

Other activities sometimes added to this standard list include:

(5) Giving money to ministry, missions, and other needs with a joyful attitude

(6) Attending a small group; or often more broadly, be part of a thriving community of other believers pursuing God and holding you accountable.

(7) Doing evangelism

A fourth tier is sometimes added that includes:

(8) Serving in the church using your time and talents

A fifth tier is sometimes attached to the fourth tier

(8a) Serving in the community

Finally, a rare sixth tier will occasionally be added:

(8b) Serving in your workplace. Usually service in the workplace is defined as doing evangelism, making money to give away, being personally ethical, or leading a small group (This is more of a variation of 1–7 in a new location.)

This list includes great spiritual formation activities that we should all practice. However, in most cases, they are presented as a hierarchy in which reflective activities are in the highest tiers and action-oriented activities are in the lowest tiers. Also, activities located within the church building and program often ranked higher in emphasis and importance than activities located in the community or workplace.

This informal, unspoken hierarchy is so strongly a part of our Christian teaching that we would never dare to ask the question, "Could service be a more vital spiritual formation activity for me than a regular quiet time, or even church attendance?" When I was a church planter, I accidentally asked this question and was surprised by the result. As I'll explain later, it should never be an "either-or" question but a "both-and" question, along with a "where do I start?" question. I've continued to ask that question in Bible studies in both urban ministry and workplace environments, and have continued to find surprising answers from both people and biblical exhortations alike.

As a church planter, I felt that I needed to develop a discipleship model that would help us create a church-wide program for making disciples. I researched the topic and concluded most Protestant churches have a similar model of how disciples are made. The model seems to have been influenced by 17th- and 18th-century Puritan writers. I scribed a simple synthesis of this view:

First, God inspires people to be motivated to grow.

Second, a person's mind is changed.

Third, the changed mind changes the heart. A person's emotions and sentiments are changed.

Fourth, the person's will is changed. He or she wants to do differently.

Fifth, the person's actions are changed. He or she acts differently.

I drew the chart to look like this:

inspiration

mind ——————> heart ——————> will ——————> action

As a pastor, I thought I needed to line up the primary programs and activities of the church with this sequence. What does the church do to help people move along this flow from inspiration to changed actions?

First, prayer, worship, and preaching open a person up to hear God inspire them to change. Worship helps them hear God's power and love. Preaching helps them hear God's conviction.

Second, teaching helps their minds learn about God, the Bible, church tradition, and how their thinking must change.

Third, small groups, pastoral care, counseling, and fellowship activities provide a place for stories to be told, burdens to be lifted, and lives to be touched in ways that engage the emotions.

Fourth, discipleship groups that focus on spiritual disciplines and lay mobilization programs help people make commitments to engage the will to do what the heart is leading the will to do.

Fifth, ongoing service programs inside the church, in the community, in the marketplace and in global missions provide vehicles for people to continue in the changed actions to which their minds, hearts, and wills have led them.

I added these church programs to the chart so it now looked like:

inspiration

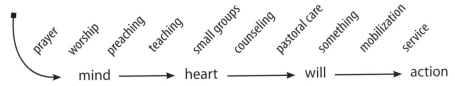

After doing this, I thought it might be good to actually ask people what church activities God was using most in their lives. I assumed many would say worship services, and that my sermons were most instrumental in their growth—or at least started their growth. That would certainly be the conclusion from *my* chart. Instead, I heard many people say they grew spiritually more through *doing* service activities than listening to my sermons each Sunday. (Many were new Christians and didn't realize the rule about making sure their senior pastor feels he really is the center of the world.) It was a bit humbling, but I realized that what they were saying had actually been true for me my whole life.

Green Lights for Growth

Sermons and worship experiences in my life were like revving an engine on a fast car. They created in me a knowledge and potential for spiritual formation. They motivated me. They warmed up my spiritual-growth engine and got me ready to move toward obedience. However, if the sermons and worship were not quickly connected to service experiences in the community or my workplace, they rarely created the obedience and spiritual growth they were intended to create. As a result, I ended up impressing others with all the noise and smoke I could make, but didn't move very far.

For me, real spiritual growth movement occurred when I was called to do something with all that accumulated knowledge. The worship and sermons were necessary, but the actual growth didn't occur until service activities put the transmission into gear and the engine became connected to the wheels.

After hearing this, I also started thinking about how people learn and how they change. I had heard a general statement during teaching research that 50 percent of the world learns deductively—moving from abstract theory to concrete application. This is sometimes called academic learning since most universities start with theory and move toward application in many of their subjects. I also had heard that the other 50 percent of the world learns inductively—first doing concrete actions and skills, then asking later the "why" behind the "what" that they have learned. This is called apprentice or agricultural learning since, for many centuries, most people had their parents or other adults show them what to do. Then when their skills were honed, they would explain why they were doing it that way.

The chart I had drawn made sense for academic learners, but did it make sense for apprentice learners? In my studies of spiritual formation, I also recognized many of the Catholic approaches started from the opposite side of my chart. This approach looked like:

inspiration

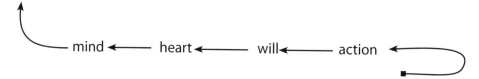

First, serve others or practice disciplines in a way that these become life-habits.

Second, as an action becomes a habit, it becomes something that your will is both confident in doing, and desires to do.

Third, as your will increases its desire to do something well, your emotions and sentiments join in and now it is something that gives you great joy, satisfaction, and excitement to do. You begin to serve and pursue spiritual disciplines not just from habit, but from a deep sense of joy in doing them.

Fourth, as your heart is open, you find your mind constantly thinking about the things that bring joy to your heart. You want to study these things more and learn as much about them as is possible.

Fifth, as you understand more about what you love, you start seeing God's hand in so many places where earlier you did not see before. You recognize God's inspiration in your habits, desire of your will, love of your heart, and the knowledge of your mind.

By drawing double-sided arrows on my chart, I realized that this caught the idea that people are wired to change and grow spiritually in different directions. The new chart looked like:

inspiration

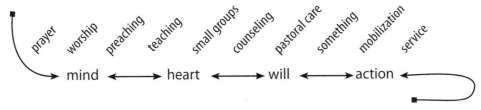

The key for my church was to make sure that we had programs to support this whole process, no matter which way a person was heading into spiritual formation. I needed to make sure there were easy entry points for people at both ends. For some, the journey in our community started in the worship service. For others, the journey in our community started when we visited the prisons. Still others seemed to find their start in our small groups.

In reality, most of us want to engage in church programs that make us *think* or *feel* we are growing spiritually, but we don't want to commit to things that will actually *change* us. The temptation for academic learners: to engage in programs only on the left side of the chart. The temptation for apprentice learners: to be involved in programs only on the right side of the chart. But if people did not engage in all aspects of growth, they could fool themselves. They could believe that because they knew something in their heads, or did something with their hands, they had fully changed. The job of my church then was to track, mentor, motivate, and push people to become involved in the full activities of the chart.

The question I then learned to ask was not, "Is a quiet time more important than service, or is service more important than a quiet time?" The better question is, "Are you doing both prayer and service?" If you are most comfortable with one and are doing it well, then how can I help you do more the one that you are least comfortable with? If a strong prayer life is not creating a greater desire to serve, then it is worth asking, why? If service activities are not creating a greater thirst for prayer, Bible study, and church attendance, then it is time to make a change in the focus and motive of those service activities.

This doesn't mean that all of us live on both sides of the chart equally. God made some of us more reflective and others more action-oriented. God-given wiring means that we will probably be spiritually formed the most when we practice spiritual formation activities that are most consistent with that wiring. However, that is not an excuse to say, "I don't do windows." Discipleship by its nature is a call outside of our comfort zone.

More importantly, pastors and church leaders need to make sure they are creating a spiritual growth community that has entry points for all types of people, and that regardless of their own style, they value and respect the God-given spiritual growth styles of others. When someone says, "Pastor, I pray more fervently when I am serving in the prisons than when you lead us in corporate prayer," leaders should not take that as a statement about their shortcomings. Or if someone says, "When I am with non-Christians who ask questions about God,

I feel more connected to God than at any worship service," that doesn't mean the worship services are poorly led. Instead, it provides another avenue for leaders to encourage the work of the church *scattered* as they provide primary leadership to the church *gathered*.

Unfortunately, many churches elevate preaching or worship as keys to spiritual formation, while community and service are seen as lesser activities. To put all these activities on the same level is probably too radical for most churches. Yet I have found that for people who are in urban ministry, there is something freeing about realizing that serving the least, the last, and the lost is not an after-thought in spiritual formation. Many people are wired by God from birth in a way that serving the poor is the entry point that God planned for them in order to draw them into a much larger adventure in growing closer to God. Serving the poor is a powerful spiritual formation activity, but it is not the only gateway of service to activate spiritual formation.

Many current movements in global Christianity are opening up new avenues of deep spiritual formation for people who spend most of their lives serving in the workplace. A call to business is increasingly seen not as a second-class calling. Ministry in the workplace is being redefined to embrace much more than just "church-like" activities that are practiced at work. People are beginning to see grateful attitudes toward God during their work as a form of prayer. Some understand the purposeful application of their God-given gifts in work is a form of worship—ascribing worth and praise to God for how He created them. Others are able to see the product of their work as participating in the stewardship of the earth to display God's purpose in the world, and remind fellow employees that they are made in God's image. These new perspectives in the workplace do not shortchange the work of proclaiming the good news of Jesus Christ's death and resurrection for the saving of souls for eternity. Instead, they display the result of this good news in all aspects of daily life, opening up doors for people to see and hear the fullness of the gospel.

So a first conclusion about what would improve spiritual formation and discipleship in our churches is to place the activities of service in the commu-nity, world, or workplace higher in the list of priorities of the church. Reflective activities need to be better connected to action activities, and action activities need to be more strongly connected to reflective activities. But even a healthy connection between the head-heart-hands spiritual formation activities does not always result in vibrant spiritual growth.

What About the Motive?

In most cases, the topic of spiritual formation doesn't just cover the activities of spiritual formation, but also its motives. I've watched many people do a wide variety of spiritual formation activities very well, but many did not end up with what looked like well-formed spiritual lives. I have often been surprised to meet people who had very extensive quiet times, but who were proud, hard, and even mean toward others. They behaved impeccably, but they were not much fun to be around. And then a few of them suddenly went off the deep end; had an affair, renounced their faith, and disappeared from the church community. The conclusion is that right activities with wrong motives will not result in spiritual formation.

The problem is that it is hard to understand motives, especially if you are wired as an action-oriented person. Motives are easy to judge in others but very tricky to unearth in ourselves. Jeremiah 17:9 says, "The heart is deceitful above all things, and desperately sick. Who can understand it?" Traditional spiritual formation was often connected to a spiritual director. I've been trained as both a spiritual director and a basic counselor and, while the language of each is very different, the approaches are surprisingly similar. By asking questions, drawing out stories of childhood and current pain, and exploring emotions, motives can be slowly unearthed.

I've also discovered that action-oriented urban ministers may be often trained as counselors but tend to avoid the professional-counseling couch like the plague. Perhaps the Hollywood image of tough-guy Tony Soprano on a psychiatrist's couch will open up this important vehicle for spiritual formation more. But because of finances or stereotypes, most people in urban ministry will choose to explore motives through other avenues.

What Is the Goal of Spiritual Formation?

During the mid-1980s, I was hired to start a spiritual formation program at a large seminary. After a few years, we had about 600 students in the program, all committed to spending 90 minutes each week for two years in the same small group, exploring their spiritual growth. Faculty or peer mentors who were very godly led the small groups, but the program was too large to give each leader extensive training in either spiritual direction or counseling.

So instead of a counseling process to uncover the motives of our hearts, we started a less direct process of seeking out motives by simply asking, "What is the goal of your spiritual formation?" Another way of asking the same thing is, "What would you look like if you were more spiritually formed?" As easy as this question sounds, it is very confusing to most of us.

Since we were in a seminary environment, we found people tended to give us impersonal and often philosophical answers. So we learned to ask the same question in still another way: "Who is the holiest person you've met?" Since only God is holy and even the best of us are light years away from holy, the question forced a conversation where even the most impressive spiritual disciplines seemed futile. The stories also revealed amazing people who were not impressive so much by their great disciplines, their great works, or even their fame, but by their simple, profound, and consistent trust in God. It was these stories that revealed much about the one true goal of all spiritual formation activities. Once you know a simple goal, it is so much easier to simplify and prioritize the various activities and pathways that lead to that goal.

The One Thing of Spiritual Formation

In the 1991 movie *City Slickers*, actor Billy Crystal plays the character Mitch, who is having a midlife crisis, trying to "find himself" on a dude ranch. His guide, Curly, says in a gruff voice, "Do you know what the secret of life is? Mitch replies, "No, what?" Curly replies, "One thing. Just one thing. You stick to that and everything else don't mean [nothing]."

As I listened to the students' stories, it suddenly became clear what the *one thing* of spiritual formation is. To understand, we first have to start with the core of the problem that spiritual formation is trying to solve.

The problem is that we are cynical, or at least skeptical, of God's character. We come by it naturally. We are born that way. It was actually Eve and Adam who started this skepticism. They believed Satan when he planted the seed of doubt about God in their minds. In Genesis 3:4–5, Satan says, "You will not surely die . . . For God knows that when you eat of it your eyes will be opened, and you will be like God, knowing good and evil." My paraphrase is something like, "Oh, come on. You don't believe that baloney do you? You see, God is holding out. He has His best interest in mind, but not yours. If you do eat of it, then you will be like God and he doesn't want you competing with him. Go ahead and eat it. Take control of your own destiny. You know what's best for you. Don't trust God to look out for you. Look out for number-one yourself."

As a result, self-dependence is the essence of our fleshly rebellion against God and our continuing skepticism of His character. We don't really believe we can make our lives work the way we desire, but we certainly don't think anyone else, even God, cares enough about us to do it better than ourselves. So to be a fallen human means we manipulate, scramble, scrape, lie to ourselves, become addicted, or live in a fantasy world to make our lives work. It is a painful existence, but we really think our pitiful answer is the best there is. Some of us think God is strong enough to fix things, but think that He doesn't seem to be doing it in a way that fits our plan and our timetable. Rather than depend on Him, at least we know where we stand and what *we* can do.

The core problem is skepticism about God's character. As a result, our core pursuit is independence of God. The "one thing" that should be the focus of all spiritual formation is to build increasing trust of God's character. The more honest we are about our cynicism toward God, the more the goal of our spiritual formation activities can be clear. We pray not to "earn brownie points," so God will do what we want. We pray to learn that God is the Creator, and we are the creatures, and this arrangement is a good thing. We don't worship in church to get an emotional fix to last us until the next Sunday. We worship God to put ourselves in a place where we, as a community, help each other agree about God's power and goodness and our lack of both. We study the Bible not to be inspired by great men and women like King David, Mary Magdalene, Priscilla, or the Apostle Paul. The Bible is not a book to learn the tricks of how to manipulate God and force Him to bless our lives. The Bible shows us repeatedly the faithful character of God, and most often, the unfaithful character of men and women like us, who still are deeply cared for by God in spite of themselves.

Using Spiritual Formation Activities to Avoid Spiritual Formation

So if our core problem is skepticism about God and our core pursuit is independence, it shouldn't surprise us that we all have a tendency to take something very good such as spiritual formation activities and use them to increase our self-sufficiency. As a result, spiritual formation becomes very complicated and difficult. We pursue spiritual disciplines, correct doctrine, and right behavior as a way to "white knuckle" ourselves to maturity. The very means by which God intended to increase our trust in His character are hijacked to increase our trust in our own abilities.

If we have been a Christian for a long time, our skepticism may be all the more hidden from us because our minds and our words assert trust of God. The more we define spiritual formation as right thinking, right words, and right behaviors that are "better than most," the more likely we are to use spiritual formation activities to hide the real issues of skepticism in our hearts. The goal becomes looking right, not being right. The focus becomes the activities, not the motives. The means replace the goal. We may think that to be spiritually formed is to be contemplative, or disciplined, or knowledgeable, or passionless. These are great means, but they are not the goal. If this happens, we'll end up giving credit to God in our words and in our conscious thoughts, but keeping the deepest motives of our heart firmly fixed on making sure we are the captains of our own ship.

The frightening conclusion is that the *exact same* great spiritual formation activities could be used to either cause us to grow or to cause us to avoid growth while fooling ourselves and others at the same time.

One of the great classics of science fiction is the movie *Aliens*. In the movie, horribly ugly alien creatures take over the bodies of humans and feed off of them to accomplish the aliens' foul deeds. I've watched the movie many times and always side with the humans as they fight seemingly impossible odds to overcome these insidious body snatchers. Yet, in the realm of spiritual formation, my heart is actually the alien taking over the body of God-given spiritual formation activities to use them for my foul purposes. I wish it weren't true. I wish these activities had their own special powers so that if I just did them, all would be well. But the power is not in the activities, but in the motive of the heart. And the motive of the heart is where I find I deceive myself the most. I feel as Paul does when he cries out in Romans 7:24, "What a wretched man I am! Who will rescue me from this body of death?"

The answer to Paul's cry is, of course, in verse 25: "Thanks be to God—through Jesus Christ our Lord!" The true goal of spiritual maturity is greater trust and dependence on God. I cannot accomplish this without God's power. And, this increased trust will naturally result in increased godly behavior that comes *from* the heart, not a veneer spiritually that comes from white-knuckling my way through spiritual disciplines.

Lessons We Can Learn

The first lesson we can learn from this is that those of us who lead organizations such as churches, universities, businesses, or urban ministries need to force more reflective time into our lives. There is no way we can be spiritually formed if we don't make daily, weekly, monthly, quarterly, and yearly set-aside times for prayer and the core disciplines of spiritual formation.

The second lesson we can learn from this may appear to contradict the first. We can't delegate spiritual formation as activities that are only practiced in retreat and reflection settings. We need to pursue spiritual formation in ways that are consistent with how God has made us. Many people in urban ministry are action-oriented. We jump in to meet a need rather than reflect on why the need is there. Rather than be ashamed of how God has made us, we need to find intentional ways to pray, reflect, worship, and discover biblical truth on the front lines of our work and ministry.

The third lesson we can learn from this is that our motives are flawed and deceitful, but this doesn't drive God away. We need to be honest about how deeply cynical we are and how much we cannot succeed in spiritual formation no matter how hard we work. Our hope is not how fast we can confess or get "Jesus back on the throne" of our life, as if we need to convince God not to give up on us. If the goal of spiritual formation were correct behavior, our sin would demonstrate our failure in spiritual formation. But if the true goal of spiritual formation is increased trust in God, actually our failure can be an amazing opening to growth. When we fail, we don't have to scramble to cover our failure. Our first reaction should *not* be to run to a 1 John 1:9 formula to impress God with the sincerity and speed of our confession.

The first step should be to say, "God, once again, my sin demonstrates that You are holy and I am not. No matter how hard I try, I cannot do this by myself. Thank You that You have given me forgiveness, and in spite of how inconsistent I am, You are always consistent in Your goodness. Now, let me confess . . . or recommit . . . or be reminded. . . ."

As the goal of spiritual formation is clear, it also allows more simplicity in our journey; more flexibility in how we arrange the means of spiritual formation in our lives; and more confidence that we will be formed by God, in part now, and fully for eternity in heaven.

■ ■ ■ Personal Reflection

Think about the times in your life when you felt you were growing the most spiritually. What was present in your life at that time? One or more close relationships? A teacher? A trial? Corporate worship? Particular disciplines? An opportunity to serve others?

In what activities do you participate in your church now that seem to cause the greatest spiritual growth?

Is there anything in this chapter that helps explain this in your life?

■ ■ ■ Bible Reflection

As you read James 1–2:
What surprised you about this and the previous chapter? What was encouraging? What was convicting?

James 2:14 and 2:24 are sometimes confusing. The point is not that works are required for a person to go to heaven, but that true faith—and not only claimed faith—is evidenced by works. It is the true faith, not the works, that saves a person. Why do you think it is so important for us to understand the difference between faith by words only, and faith confirmed by actions?

How do you see evidence in your own life of faith confirmed by actions?

Chapter Ten: GOD'S PRIORITY FOR URBAN MINISTRY

Theme: Urban ministry draws us into pain, presence, power, and plurality in order to increase our dependency upon God and others.

Bible Reading
Acts 2:42–47
Hebrews 10:22–25

Review of Key Themes

People often think *urban* means inner city: ghettos, at-risk youth, high crime, and economic disparity. *Urban* includes and goes far beyond these. *Urban* means *a location* that includes business and government centers, both poor and wealthy neighborhoods, and diverse cultures with dense populations. The urban environment is today's cultural center, producing whole new leadership styles, perspectives, and lifestyles that have dominated media, music, and fashion. Urban challenges require a different kind of leadership than what was required only a few short years ago.

Yet, *urban* doesn't just mean a location, but also *a mind-set* and perspective. The influence of this mind-set is sometimes called *urbanization*. The urban mind-set is increasingly influencing ways people in rural, suburban, and nomadic geographic settings think about life. The urban mind-set includes:

Pluralism. An urban mind-set does not try to avoid diverse worldviews. A rural village can shape a common worldview through shared traditions, clans, and ostracizing those who don't "fit." A suburb allows people to isolate themselves in gated neighborhoods, clubs and social relationships of common mind-set. These are not options in the urban world. Urban leadership cannot overpower, ignore, or change diverse worldviews. Urban leaders live in a swirl of conflict and compromise. Collaboration is required to survive. The very process of making decisions, accomplishing tasks, forming relationships and living life takes on a multicultural complexity.

Pain. An urban mind-set forces people to look hard into the pain of what it means to be human in a fallen world. Attempts to recreate a human-engineered garden of Eden fail more readily in urban settings. The harshness of urban life forces acknowledgement of the realities of life that everyone faces, but that some have the resources, isolation, and power to avoid facing head-on.

Presence. An urban setting doesn't allow for as much space between people as the suburbs do, creating an urban mind-set that doesn't allow people to retreat and reappear with masks. Authenticity is not optional since fakery is too easily uncovered. Life is raw and fast, not allowing time for collected wits or subdued emotions. People value relationships, not polished strategies.

Power. An urban mind-set talks about power in open terms: the lack of it, the acquisition of it, and the healthy stewardship of it. Power is vividly understood politically, economically, socially, and personally. People who don't have ready access to power are much more aware of power than those who have the privilege to take power for granted. In an urban mind-set, ministry often doesn't occur until power is gained, then given in order to empower someone else.

Rural and suburban communities face these same issues, but in lesser degrees. The concentrated dose of these core realities make the urban world the crucible from which all other cultures are influenced and new styles of leadership first emerge. The urban world today is what much of the rest of the world will face tomorrow.

Some other reoccurring urban themes include:

Urban as Global Diversity

In the United States, the poorest neighborhoods are often in the inner core of a city. Yet, in many other cities of the world, the city core is where the wealthy live while the poor live on the outskirts. Many US cities are seeing regentrification in their downtown cores and the new ghettos of large apartment complexes are emerging in the first ring of freeways. *City* is not just poor and powerless, but also rich and powerful. *City* is not just social work, but also business growth, engineering infrastructure, political influence, education, health care, zoning, art, environment; all connected to diverse local and international constituencies. The old narrow stereotypes of the poverty-stricken inner city ghetto are increasingly creating blindness to system-wide issues.

Yet the heart of urban ministry remains in the hands of those who live with and who pastor the poor. The urban pastor and the urban worker have significant callings, even though so much of their day-to-day work seems so futile. The city is where the whole world breathes in and breathes out. Nations migrate through the city. A faithful worker in the city can literally have an impact on the whole world through migratory streams, immigrant's connections to their families in other continents, and through developing street-smart leaders who will lead world mission of the future. There is a constant theme of raising the head of the urban worker to see how vital their role is to the whole system of mission God has created.

The City as Carnival of Common Grace

For many, the mind-set of urban ministry is "how can we fix the problem?" Traditional approaches to urban ministry assume that outsiders must come in and "save" the poor and helpless people of the city because they cannot help themselves. In contrast, new approaches called "asset-based community development" (ABCD) start with the assumption that most of the solutions reside in the creativity, leadership, and resources of those already living in the community. There also is a strong theological perspective to this approach. It is assumed that the Holy Spirit is already at work in the place of greatest poverty long before we arrive. God is at work redeeming what appear to be even the most corrupt government structures, the most greed-ridden businesses, and those groups involved in the most desperate of cultural clashes. Often God's work is hindered not by our lack of effort, but by our inattention to see God's previous and ongoing work, in our zeal to pursue our own solutions.

How then does it make a difference if you see the city not as a problem to be fixed, but as a work of God to be experienced and explored? One of the foundational methodologies that Ray Bakke pioneers is "the city consultation." These consultations use a simple, but relationship-intense method. Before conducting a city consultation, Ray would make sure the key business, government, education, church (Protestant, Catholic, and Orthodox) and nonprofit leaders of the city dedicate up to four days to spend together. Then with this "captured audience" of the key leaders of a city, the consultation would *not*:

- use the platform to spend long hours in lectures.
- develop a comprehensive inventory of the needs and problems of the city.
- impose a "one-size-fits-all" strategy for city transformation.

Instead, the consultation would ask the simple question, "What are the signs of hope in your city?" For Christians, the same question might be phrased. "What evidence can you show me that demonstrates God is active and present in this city?" Then people would start telling each other story after story of God's work. At the end of the consultation, people leave, not overwhelmed with the problems of the city but more emboldened by the God of their city. They leave more aware of God's abiding presence. The ongoing plans, projects, and organizations that result from the consultations start with the hope that comes from awareness that participants are joining a work of God that was already in process.

People over Programs

City workers face myriad complex issues. The temptation when the puzzle is overwhelming and we don't know where to start is to make ourselves busy with programs. Effective urban ministry must start with *relationships* and let the programs emerge slowly—often inefficiently—from the relationships. What looks like a slow, wandering, unimpressive, "slow-turtle" beginning often results in a long-term effectiveness that far surpasses the "fast-start rabbit" programmatic false starts that tempt us to mimic.

It is tempting to do urban ministry either by long-distance planning or frenetic action. Yet it never works without the slow, seemingly inconsequential, incarnational presence with and among the people. Nothing substitutes for presence—physical, emotional, spiritual, and vulnerable connection with people in cultures dissimilar to our own.

Give Away the Decisions

Many people reading this book have access to higher education, power and resources. It is easy in that position to become a well-intentioned, decision-making hog. To counter that constant temptation, we must understand an image-bearer theology:

(a) God made *all* people in His image.

(b) Part of what this means is that we are to represent God on this earth—to steward God's creation in response to God's direction. We are the face or image of God to His creation. We are creatures designed to work God's garden and to make decisions about God's creation.

(c) While the fall of Genesis 3 caused us to lose much of the connection that God intended, we are still decision-making creatures. All of us—even nonChristians—find joy and fulfillment as we take responsibility and make decisions for God's creation.

(d) One of the best ways to empower others is to give them the power to make decisions, even if those decisions are not exactly how we would do things. It is important to educate, coach, and lead by example, but not actually take away others' power to decide. By not making decisions on others' behalf, we are encouraging them to live increasingly as image-bearers themselves. For many, being respected as an image-bearer is the route that leads to reconnection with God.

People with power and resources, who make all the decisions because they think they know best, may improve short-term conditions but reap great long-term damage. Good urban ministry cannot violate timeless biblical image-bearer theology.

God Has Revealed Himself in History

Much about God can be discovered in God's interaction with people and places in the past. To dismiss the history of the church, or the history of a place, or the history of an idea is to arrogantly dismiss God's amazing work throughout the centuries. History holds the clues to the present and future. Planning for the future without first researching the past is planting a tree without roots—it will stay green for a short season, then wither.

God Is Shaking Up the World

Almost every city in the world is experiencing tumultuous change. Nations are migrating to the cities. The world is facing a move from rural to urban in cataclysmic ways. The world has never been so connected together by technology. New countries are growing up fast and ancient cultures are facing new identity crises. Isolation in an attempt to reclaim a past glory is no longer an option.

The city is not a mosaic that assumes the pieces are static and can be captured once-for-all into a comprehensive picture. It is a massive, fast-turning, kaleidoscope of interesting sights, sounds, and smells. The view changes constantly. The enjoyment is studying every nook and cranny, and then going back again to discover how it has changed.

Public Theology

Public theology is about how each of us, our churches, and organizations can obey God's call for us to transform the place where we live. Much of our time and energy is consumed by our own needs, our family's activities, and the programs of our own church. Unless we are intentional, we can live much of our lives focusing on our own needs. Yet God calls us to be outward people—reaching out to people unlike ourselves. God calls us to be public people—living lives that shine like a city on a hill rather than hidden under a bushel. God calls us to be compassionate people—feeding the hungry, giving to the poor, and visiting the prisoners.

Urban Ministry as Discipleship

The odd thing about obeying God is that, at first, it seems like a detour from what we want, but ends up being the only way to truly achieve what we want. Mission is the very thing that helps us move away from a consumer mind-set of selfish needs toward a discipleship mind-set of God's desires and blessing.

Many people begin urban ministry as a way to help others. As they stay in it over the long haul, they find that it has become their own salvation—a means to avoid addictions to consumer lifestyles, ever-expanding materialism, and ever-present selfishness. Many will say that the city has become the place where they are transformed from consumers to disciples; from people seeking personal fulfillment to people who know their blessings.

Pluralism, pain, presence, and power—these are four "P's" along with the eight themes we have covered that I hope you can use as a mental filing cabinet to help you remember and connect the stories, illustrations, biblical insights, and teaching of *City Signals*.

■ ■ ■ Personal Reflection

Which of the four "P's" and eight themes are confirmations of what you've learned in your own urban ministry journey?

Which are new themes?

What would you add to these?

■ ■ ■ Bible Reflection

Read Acts 2:42–47 and Hebrews 10:22–25
List out the characteristics found in the community described in these two passages.

Where in your life is a community that is closest to what is described in these two passages?

CITY SIGNALS

Principles and Practices for **Ministering in Today's Global Communities**

by Brad Smith

LEADER'S GUIDE

For use with *City Signals* Leader Kit DVDs by Ray Bakke

Leader's Guide FOR GROUP STUDY OF CITY SIGNALS

Introduction

Welcome to the *City Signals* study guide. This guide includes how to use *City Signals* Leader Kit DVDs with your *City Signals* study, how to best address your particular study group's learning needs, and provides chapter overviews with group discussion questions for each chapter in this book.

Each chapter correlates with a complementary DVD segment and theme. The chapters do not *repeat* the DVD content. Rather, the DVDs provide vignettes of various aspects of urban ministry to enhance study. The DVDs in the *Leader's Kit* provide a total of 10 approximately 25-minute segments that feature urbanologist, missiologist, and acclaimed Bible teacher Ray Bakke. Bakke shares about the core principles of urban ministry. Used together with this *City Signals* group study guide, the study prepares minds and hearts for what God has in store for urban ministers.

As the group leader, you have a great deal of freedom to manipulate what you have here to best fit the needs of your group. The group study structure is flexible; pull out and rearrange the book chapters and DVD viewing opportunities in the order that best serves your group. The first eight segments of the DVDs and this book focus on the theology, principles, and practices of global urban ministry. The last two DVD segments, *Saints in Cities: An Urban Family Album of the Past 2000 Years*, provides a whirlwind tour of the urban themes in church history as told through key personalities in that history; A.D. 33 to A.D. 1300, and A.D. 1300 to the present.

What Does the Title *City Signals* mean?

Two quick answers:

(1) The nations reveal God and global cities reveal the nations.

(2) God has called us to witness to the nations. Today that calling can be part of your everyday life more than ever before,

Structuring Your Study

It is often beneficial for a group to "form and norm" through sharing stories before launching into what is known as the "storm" stage of interaction and diverse thinking about subject matter. Chapter one of this book is designed to help launch the group before the first DVD session.

Most groups will find it helpful thereafter to read the book chapters and study related Bible passages noted in the chapters before attending group meetings. Groups can view DVD content either before the group meeting to allow more group discussion time, or in the group so DVD content is fresh in everyone's mind.

The structure of both the DVD series and book can be summarized as follows:

	City Signals book Theme		*City Signals Leader Kit* DVD theme
1	**Our Story in the City:** Spiritual formation starts with God's story of joy and brokenness in our own life	1	**A World in Motion:** Large cities are the hubs of tumultuous worldwide migration streams. The center of the church is moving beyond North America.
2	**Big World, Big God:** The turmoil of global urban diversity opens us to have a bigger view of God.	2	**How Cities Challenge Churches:** New challenges and structures in the city require new structures in the church.

	City Signals book theme		*City Signals* Leader Kit DVD theme
3	**Changing World, Changing Church:** God forms us through the church, but it may be a different form of *church* than what we expect.	3	**The Making of a World-Class City:** Cities have unique histories that form unique personalities. We must contextualize our work to the unique culture of the city.
4	**God Is Already Present:** We grow as we discern and follow where God has preceded us.	4	**The Nations Are in the Neighborhood:** The example of Chicago's ethnic history and diversity demonstrates the impact of power and money on cities.
5	**Working with Fire:** God calls us to steward money and power as we serve the poor and the powerful.	5	**Ghetto as a Money Sieve:** Programs without Empowerment: A Chicago urban example illustrates the priority of giving people the power to make their own decisions.
6	**Give Away Rights:** God calls us to give away our right to make the decisions to those whom we serve.	6	**Reading the City, Unearthing the Treasures of a Neighborhood:** Getting to know the place where you minister by intentional research, relationships, and commitments.
7	**Incarnational Presence:** God forms us when we commit to relationships among the least, the last, and the lost.	7	**Transforming the City (Four Examples in Africa):** Holistic urban ministry preaches the gospel, serves the poor, and influences the powerful.
8	**Whole Gospel:** Contrast between Islam and Christian urban ministries in Africa	8	**Transforming the City (Examples in North America):** Stories of various commitments people have made that God has used to transform cities.
9	**Hands, Heart, and Head Formation:** The goal of spiritual formation is to increase our trust and dependence on God as the deepest motives of our hearts.	9	**Diognetus to Dominic:** 1,200 Years of Urban Ministry
10	**God's Priority for Urban Ministry:** Urban ministry draws us into pain, presence, power, and plurality, in order to increase our dependency on God and others.	10	**Savonarola to Florence to Teresa of Calcutta:** Models of Urban Reform

Feel free to pull out and rearrange the chapters into the order that best serves your group.

Before you embark on this study and your own life-long journey to see the world, chapter 10 of this book highlights the reoccurring themes you will see repeatedly in the book and DVDs.

Who is Ray Bakke?

From 1965 to 1968, Ray Bakke pastored Edgewater Baptist Church and from 1969 to 1979, Fairmont Avenue Baptist Church, both churches in Chicago's inner city. From 1981 to 1995, Ray was Senior Associate for Large Cities for the Lausanne Committee for World Evangelization. This work folded into the International Urban Associates Ray founded in the early nineties that merged with Bakke Graduate University (BGU) in 2005.

Ray pastored inner-city churches for 14 years. Then, for 25 years, he led 250 consultations in the largest cities of the world, bringing together business, government, church, education, and nonprofit leaders to work on issues of city transformation. For much of this time, he was either studying or teaching urban issues in various seminaries and universities. Ray's perspective is the result of 40 years of frontline experience combined with insightful reflection on the theology, principles, and practice of urban ministry.

Ray serves as the Chairman of the Board of Regents of BGU. The university provides accredited doctoral and masters degrees from the common values of urban transformation displayed by both Ray and his brother Dennis, who built a $40 billion company providing electricity to 100 million people, largely in the world's developing countries. Dennis's work in international business mirrors many of the values you will see surface through the perspective of urban ministry in the DVDs and this study. Dennis's book *Joy At Work* and its accompanying Bible Study Companion explain more about this work. BGU is currently building a business program to accompany its current urban theology programs. More information about Ray, Dennis, and the work of BGU can be found at www. bgu.edu.

People who have experienced Ray's teaching have remarked on three distinctives that have proved to be helpful to them:

Ray is practical without being prescriptive. Ray has seen the best urban ministries in 250 of the world's largest cities. This has given him a perspective that invites us all to see beyond our own tree to the great forest of God's work in the city. In turn, this gives us greater insight and confidence to innovate practice in our own setting without having to mimic someone else's program.

He is an avid reader, professor, and enthusiast for history of all kinds. Any person who has spent any time with Ray quickly gathers humorous incidents where a conversation about something trivial in the present suddenly reminds Ray about an eighth-century monk in China or a fourth-century theological argument in Northern Africa.

Ray is known for his biblical teaching that opens new insights into familiar scriptures from a global, urban, missions-centered theme. God allows Ray to open up scriptures in new ways even for long-time Bible students who have read a particular Scripture 100 times, but have missed the insight that jumps out like a neon sign to an urban theologian.

What approach should I take with my group?

This study can be part of a weekly small-group time, an all-day leaders' retreat, an educational course, or part of a personal study program.

Each of the 10 chapters includes:

(1) Bible passages to read;

(2) study material that can be used either as a preview or review of 25-minute DVD sessions;

(3) questions for personal reflection;

This study guide provides:

(4) small-group discussion questions.

How Do I Use This Guide?

There are many ways to use the Bible study and DVD together as already stated. The Bible passages and study chapters can be read either before or after watching the DVD, depending if you want a preview or a review of the DVD. All except the group discussion questions can be done before the group meeting in order to use the full group time for discussion questions. Or you can watch the DVD together, then read the Bible passages and study guide together and then immediately answer the discussion questions—all during group time.

For both group and individual study, you may find it most helpful to write out the answers to the personal reflection questions in each chapter so you can refer back to them when you get to the discussion questions.

Preparing to Lead the Study

Step 1:

List what you think are the needs of your group:

Does your group have novice or advanced experience with or knowledge of urban ministry? Do they already know and trust each other, or are they a new group? What have they told you are the needs they have and the hopes they have for how this group will meet their needs?

Step 2:

Then list the goals you have for this study. Is your primary goal to:

(a) expose people to some basic scriptural concepts, experiences, and principles of urban ministry

(b) bond the group to a deeper level of conversation, trust, and camaraderie

(c) motivate people to get excited about urban ministry

(d) help a group of action-oriented doers to slow down and reflect as a group on Scripture and their deeper motives

Step 3:

List what parameters you have:

Are you preparing for a short-term missions trip and have only three to four sessions in which to do a preparation group study?

Are you an ongoing small group or staff team and have the flexibility to cover all 10 segments plus a retreat to share life maps?

Are you a professor in a university program and you can assign students to do whatever part of this study you want them to do and they'll do it (you wish!)?

How often will your group meet (weekly, biweekly, monthly, in a retreat setting)?

How much time will members truly commit to prepare before group discussion?

How much time will you have for group discussion?

How much time do you want to take for group prayer, small talk, teaching new content, or walking through this material before each group discussion?

Do you want group members to spend some time after the group discussion writing in their journals or doing additional work to help them reflect upon the discussion?

How will you use the DVD and chapters before each group meeting:

(a) All reading and DVD watching will take place before the group meeting so that group time can focus only on discussion.

(b) Everyone reads the chapter before the group time, but the group watches the DVD together then discusses both.

(c) Everyone watches the DVD before the group time, then reads the chapter together and then goes through the questions as a group.

(d) One person either reads the chapter or watches the DVD before the group time, the shares snippets of the DVD or quotes from the study guide for the group to respond to and discuss.

(e) Some weeks you use the DVD, and some weeks you use a chapter before group time depending upon what is most pertinent to the group.
How many weeks do you have to do this study?

Step 4:

Make a quick chart that includes the weeks you will meet, like this:

	Pre-reading	Pre-watching	Prayer/teaching	Group discussion	Post-work
Week #s					

Step 5:

Watch the DVD series and skim through this study guide on your own. The outline table in the introduction can provide a navigation aid as you do this. Assume you have 21 tools (10 DVD segments + 10 study guide segments + 1 life map exercise) that you can use to whatever degree you want. The DVD series and chapters are in an order that generally build upon each other, but they can be separated and used individually or reassembled in an order that may make more sense to your group. Decide which segments are most pertinent to your group. Decide which ones should come first given your group's needs and previous exposure then fill in the chart with the combination and order that works best for you. No matter how you arrange the studies and DVDs it probably makes sense to start with the study guide chapter one since it encourages your group to start with a culture of story-telling and exploring heart motives.

OR You can replace steps 1–5 with:

Week 1: Get your group in the same room. Read chapter 1 together and answer the questions.

Week 2: Get your group in the same room. View DVD 1, 25 minutes. Read chapter 2 together and answer the questions.

Week 3: Get your group in the same room. Turn on DVD 2 for 25 minutes. Read chapter 3 together and answer the questions. (etc.)

You can also replace the questions at the end of any of the chapters with:

(1) What did you read in the chapter or see in the DVD that

(a) surprised you?

(b) you thought was helpful?

(c) that you disagree with?

(d) that was a new thought to you?

(e) that reminds you of something you experienced?

(2) Is there anything you are going to do differently this week as a result of our discussion tonight?

Deeper Discussions

This study is intended to create deep sharing of personal hopes and fears in the midst of preparation for or participating in urban ministry. The goal is to create a safe place to explore heart motives and God's leading in the midst of ministry, for the purpose of enhancing spiritual formation—the growth toward greater trust and dependence upon God.

The study guide quickly summarizes the urban ministry principles or context to those stories. The DVDs are largely a collection of stories, often about Chicago, biblical characters, or church history. This introduces these important concepts to people who are new to urban ministry and provides a story-launching point for those who are experienced in these principles. Other sections have some original summary paragraphs that are designed to help readers launch out to new ways of thinking. As summaries, they are written to stir conversation, not to provide a balanced or in-depth presentation (i.e., a complex topic such as "Social Gospel" is synthesized in two paragraphs). It is important not to get caught up in theological or philosophical arguments, but to continue to guide the conversation toward personal feelings and application.

Levels of Communication

In small group leadership material, there is a common presentation of five levels of communication:[1]

(1) CLICHÉS—Typical, routine, oft-repeated comments, questions, and answers given out of habit. "How are you?" "Fine." "Having a good day?" "Yes."

(2) FACTS—Information/Statistics about the weather, the office, friends, the news, personal activities, etc.

(3) OPINIONS—Includes judgments, ideas, concerns, expectations, and personal goals, dreams, and desires.

(4) FEELINGS—Emotions such as fear, joy, confusion, satisfaction, or anger.

(5) NEEDS—The deepest level of communication and intimacy where you feel completely safe to reveal your unique needs with each other.

In spiritual formation, the hope is that a safe place can be achieved in the group for feelings to be expressed. Through the windows of feelings, people can learn their heart motives—what are the needs that are driving them to trust or to be skeptical

---

[1] *Adapted from "Why Am I Afraid to Tell You Who I Am?" by John Powell (Niles, IL: Argus Communications, 1969).*

of the character of God. Trust of the group is developed at the first three levels of communication which will allow levels four and five. If you move too fast, you will not reach the lower levels. If you move too slow, the group will get into the habit of keeping the conversation at the level of facts and opinions. As the group leader, you want to help the group not get stuck on levels two and three.

Some hints on how the leader can help this happen:

(1) Pray for the group individually between group meetings. Pray for specific areas of openness that you think God may be leading the person toward.

(2) Pray as a group. Set aside times each week to share prayer requests, but create boundaries so that the requests center on the needs of group members, not distant aunts facing gall-bladder surgery. Sometimes people feel awkward in just blurting out a deep feeling, but feel more comfortable sharing it as a prayer request.

(3) Talk less and ask more questions.

(4) When you do talk, share more about your feelings than your opinions. Spend more time telling stories of your failures and confusions than stories of your successes. Try to share one level deeper than the current norm of the group so they can follow your lead to deeper discussion.

(5) If you find everyone is talking to you as the group leader and not to each other, cut off eye contact so they are forced to look to someone else to get eye contact. Or ask another group member to respond with what they feel about what another member just said. Ask them to speak directly to the person they are responding to.

(6) Make sure everyone agrees confidentiality. What is said in the group stays in the group.

Chapter Overviews and Group Discussion Questions

Chapter 1: Our Story in the City

Spiritual Formation Principle #1: Spiritual formation starts with God's story of joy, and brokenness in our life.

Theme: The city is an amazing place of beauty, blessing, and fulfillment for those who have ready eyes to see it that way. It is also a place that draws and forms those who are willing to explore what it means to be *broken* before God.

Bible Reading: Psalm 107

Pay particular attention to the phrases:

v.3   "those he gathered from the lands, from east and west, from north and south."

vv. 6, 13, 19, 28 "Then they cried out to the LORD in their trouble, and he delivered them from their distress."

vv. 8, 15, 21, 31 "Let them give thanks to the LORD for his unfailing love and his wonderful deeds for men,"

v. 7   "He led them by a straight way to a city where they could settle."

v. 36   "there he brought the hungry to live, and they founded a city where they could settle."

v. 43   "Whoever is wise, let him heed these things and consider the great love of the LORD."

Also read Revelation 21:1–4

Group Discussion Questions

What did you see in your study of Psalm 107 that surprised you or that you found particularly helpful?

How about Revelation 21? Since many people describe heaven as a place in the clouds or a garden, did it feel odd to picture "heaven"—the place where we will live for eternity—as a walled city?

Briefly describe your personal experience with cities. Where have you lived? Where have you worked and ministered? How has that shaped you? What do you do now with the city and why?

Look at the list of 12 reasons and motives for being involved in urban ministry. Which ones most reflect your own reasons for involvement?

(1) When in your life have you been broken before God? What did that feel like? Is it something you desire again or would rather avoid? Why?

Optional
Use the "LifeLine" or "Life Map" instructions in the appendix to tell your story to others in your group. While this is a useful exercise and will connect your group quickly, it will take at least 20 minutes for each person to talk through their life map and for the group to reflect what they identified with in the story. Your group might schedule a short retreat or extended group time to share stories.

Chapter 2: Big World, Big God
The Cities Reveal the Nations. The Nations Reveal God.

Spiritual Formation Principle #2: The turmoil of the fast changing global urban landscape opens us to have a bigger view of God.

Theme: The nations are in motion to the city. The global cities reveal the nations and the nations reveal God. God has called us to witness to the nations. Today that calling can be part of our everyday life more than ever before.

Bible Reading
Matthew 28:18–20
Acts 1:7–8
Romans 16:25–27
Revelation 7:9–10

DVD Session 1: A World in Motion

Group Discussion Questions
Share with your group your story and answer from the 'Personal Reflection' section.

Why do you think Revelation 7 is so explicit that people from every nation and tongue will worship God?

What do you think about living during the apex of history when the majority of the world has just started living in cities, when humankind has crossed the threshold of moving from the Garden of Genesis 1—2 to the City of Revelation 21—22?

Share your answers to question #3 in the Bible Reflection section. Do you feel any increasing sense in your life to be more proactive in pursuing cross-cultural mission experiences—either in your own city, in a city in your nation, or abroad?

Chapter 3: Changing World, Changing Church

Spiritual Formation Principle #3: God forms us through His church, but it may be a different form of *church* than what we have been used to in the past.

Theme: The church is not a Sunday morning program in a specific building, but a community of people dependent upon God, immersed throughout the city, with the courage to face both joy and pain with deep courage.

Bible Reading
Genesis 3:14–24
Mark 8:34–38
Romans 8:18–29

DVD Session 2: How Cities Challenge Churches
New challenges and structures in the city require new structures in the church.

Group Discussion
What is one of the most painful experiences in your life that you feel free to share?

What did you discover about your character and the character of God in this experience?

Where does it feel awkward and embarrassing to share this story? Why? Where does it feel most natural to share this story? Why?

If your church is one of the more awkward places to share this, what do you think would need to happen for it to become the most natural place to share it?

Chapter 4: God Is Already Present

Spiritual Formation Principle #4: We are spiritually formed not as much by what we do and say, but how well we listen and follow where God has preceded us.

Theme: Urban ministry is less about meeting needs than it is about nurturing the strengths already present in the neighborhood.

Bible Reading
Romans 1:18–25
Hebrews 11:1–13

Ephesians 2:8–10
James 1:19–25

DVD Session 3: The Making of a World-Class City
Cities have unique histories that form unique personalities. We must contextualize our work to the unique culture of the city.

Group Discussion
Where have you seen God clearly precede your efforts in such an obvious way that it is clear you joined a work that He was already doing?

What did you do that helped you see His work? What did you do that obstructed your view of what God was already doing?

Does recognizing that God has preceded you give you greater confidence and humility as you minister in an urban community that is new to you?

How is mission and ministry strategy different when you take seriously a theology that emphasizes God's work ahead of our own? As you look at your own past efforts, with this in mind, what would you do differently?

Chapter 5: Working with Fire

Spiritual Formation Principle #5: God calls us to steward money and power as we serve the poor and the powerful in the city.

Theme: Urban ministry continues to be centered on relief and development activities, but is increasingly prioritizing advocacy for the poor.

Bible Reading
Genesis 1:26–30; 2:19–20
1 John 2:15–17

DVD Session 4: The Nations are in the Neighborhood
The example of Chicago's ethnic history and diversity demonstrates the impact of power and money on cities.

Group Discussion
What was encouraging and convicting about the Bible passages in Genesis and 1 John?

Have you ever been in a religious separatists sub-culture? What was good and bad about this experience?

What do you think are the biggest personal and public challenges you face as you pursue being a better steward for God of money, power, and sexuality?

Chapter 6: Give Away Rights

Spiritual Formation Principle #6: God calls us to give away our personal right to make decisions even if we think we know best.

Theme: Urban ministry is more about empowerment than money, solutions, or even concrete progress. Understanding past mistakes will make all the difference in how we do urban ministry today

Bible Reading
Genesis 2:19–20
Matthew 5:1-10; 6:1–4

DVD Session 5: Ghetto as a Money Sieve: Programs without Empowerment: Chicago urban example illustrates the priority of giving people the power to make their own decisions.

Group Discussion

Where have you experienced futility in suburban-urban relationships, urban ministry, relationships or work? How did you respond?

Why does Matthew 5 seem so countercultural to us—perhaps so much more so than it did 10 or 20 year ago? How much have we bought the lie of strength, self-promotion and self-expression as the primary routes to happiness?

Where can you practice the discipline of giving away decision-making authority? What do you think will happen as you do this?

Chapter 7: Incarnational Presence

Spiritual Formation Principle #7: God forms us when we commit to relationships among the least, the last and the lost.

Theme: Incarnational presence is a commitment to God's call to a place, and the relationships, circumstances and lifestyle that results from linking your present and future to the neighborhood.

Bible Reading
Matthew 25:31–46

DVD Session 6: Reading the City, Unearthing the Treasures of a Neighborhood Getting to know the place where you minister by intentional research, relationships, and commitments.

Group Discussion
Have you ever felt God's call to a specific place for a period of time? Did God also provide an unusual love and perhaps unexplainable influence in that place?

In what ways do we serve Jesus by serving the least, the last, and the lost?

Describe your present and future call to incarnational ministry among the least, the last and the lost.

Chapter 8: Whole Gospel

Spiritual Formation Principle #8: We are formed by proclaiming a gospel and living a life that reconciles us with God, ourselves, each other, and our world.

Theme: Urban ministry in hostile contexts such as Africa require presence, shrewdness, and holistic ministry.

Bible Reading
Genesis 3:1–13; 16–19
Matthew 10:16
Romans 8:12–24a

DVD Session 7: Transforming the City (Four Examples in Africa); holistic urban ministry preaches the gospel, serves the poor, and influences the powerful.

Group Discussion
How do you face pressures in your own life because you are a Christian and how does presence, shrewdness and a holistic gospel show up in how you respond to it?

What has been your understanding of the "good news" of Jesus's life, death, and resurrection? How does the discussion of the four reconciliations confirm or add to how you view this good news?

What is particularly confusing, daunting, or exciting to you about living in an era where the four aspects of the gospel are not as bifurcated as before?

Chapter 9: Hand, Heart, and Head Formation

Spiritual Formation Principle #9: Spiritual formation activities can be confusing and complicated unless we pursue them in ways that are consistent with how God has wired us, and with a focus on this one true goal of all spiritual formation activities.

Theme: The goal of spiritual formation is to increase our trust and dependence on God as the deepest motives of our hearts.

Bible Reading
James 1–2

DVD Session 8: Transforming the City (Examples in North America)
Stories of various commitments people have made that God has used to transform cities.

Group Discussion
What did you read in James 1–2 that encouraged or challenged you?

What activities in your past or in your church today most encourage you to grow spiritually? How do you think this is connected to your temperament, gifts and God-given wiring?

Chapter 10: God's Priority for Urban Ministry

Theme: Urban ministry draws us into pain, presence, power, and plurality in order to increase our dependency upon God and others.

Bible Reading
Acts 2:42–47
Hebrews 10:22–25

DVD Sessions 9–10: Diognetus to Dominic—1,200 Years of Urban Ministry and Savonarola of Florence to Teresa of Calcutta—Models of Urban Reform. A review of earlier principles, illustrated through church history for application today.

Group Discussion
How do the Acts and Hebrews passages create a hope in you for an ever-growing community with which to grow and serve?

What was the most important urban ministry principle you learned in this study?

What was the most important spiritual formation principle you learned in this study?

What have you most appreciated about the group with whom have you studied *City Signals*?

Appendix: LIFE LINE/MAP INSTRUCTIONS

The LifeLine/Map is an optional exercise for use by the individual to do a self-assessment, or by groups who want to take extra time at the beginning of this study to get to know each other more, or who want to organize a weekend retreat during the study to enhance the community bonding that is already underway.

Life Line Instructions

(1) Prepare a chronological outline of your life in five-year increments, from birth to the present. In each five-year period, list the most significant events, people, and places you experienced in your life with a one-sentence note that identifies why the event, person, or place is significant in your life.
Specifically, you are looking for:

(a) Hard Times—particularly painful events, people, or experiences

(b) High Times—things you did that gave you the sense that you were "created by God for this very purpose"

(c) Heroes—key influencers—mentors, parents, close friends, teachers; and leaders with whom you had brief exposure or even historical figures that you read about and who made an impact on you by their example

(d) Hand-of-God Events—Where did you experience unusually strong leading from God

(e) Heritage—What did you experience as part of your family tradition, church tradition, or natural gifts that influenced your life?

(2) Draw the outline onto a poster board. Create a "lifeline" that illustrates low and high points in your life. List key events, people, and experiences. Draw three lines indicating the highs and lows of your:

(a) Circumstances in your life—trials and blessings

(b) Spiritual life—your walk with God

(c) Emotions—your feelings during the times

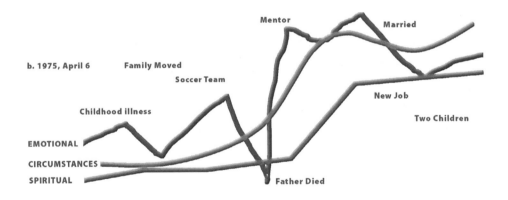

(3) Share your lifeline with your small group (10 minutes). Then answer the two questions below (5 minutes). Finally let the members of your small group reflect patterns of gifting, passion and vision that they see from your story. (5 minutes).

Report format

Tell your story, then answer the following questions.
1. What is your primary calling from God? How is that evidenced in your life, areas of interest, and gifts?

(1) Do you have a metaphor to describe how God has gifted you? (tour guide, ambassador, gardener, architect, scout, builder, etc.)

Life Map/Picture Instructions

(1) Think about your life from birth to the present. What is a picture or a metaphor that represents your life? Some ideas might include:

(a) a tree with various branches representing different times of fruitfulness or drought

(b) a landscape with mountains and valleys representing the highs and lows of your life

(c) an aerial view showing the route of your life through various stages

(d) different portraits representing the emotions, identity, relationships, and activities in your life.

(e) or a sporting event; an animal, clouds, a river, a television show or movie, a visual representation of a song, or anything that would help you tell the story of your life so far.

Specifically you are looking for:

(i) Hard Times—particularly painful events, people, or experiences

(ii) High Times—things you did that gave you the sense "you were created by God for this very purpose"

(iii) Heroes—key influencers—mentors, parents, close friends, teachers; leaders you had brief exposure to or even historical figures that you read about and were impacted by their example.

(iv) Hand of God Events—Where did you experience unusually strong leading from God

(v) Heritage—What did you experience as part of your family, church tradition, or natural gifts that influenced your life?

(2) Draw your picture onto a poster board. Include the various events of your life. Display in your picture how (a) circumstances, (b) emotions and your (c) spiritual life hits highs and lows in various times of your life.

My Life Being Revealed

(3) Share your life map in a small group (20 minutes). Then answer the two questions below (5 minutes). Finally, let the members of your small group reflect patterns of gifting, passion, and vision that they see from your story (5 minutes).

Report format

Tell your story, then answer the questions: What is your primary calling from God? How is that evidenced in your life, areas of interest, and gifts?

Make an Impact
in Your City

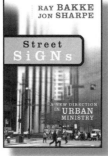
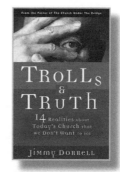
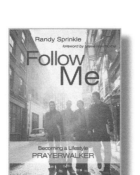

New Hope Publishers® is a division of WMU,®
an international organization that challenges Christian believers
to understand and be radically involved in God's mission.
For more information about WMU, go to www.wmu.com.
More information about New Hope books may be found at
www.newhopepublishers.com.
New Hope books may be purchased at your local bookstore.